HANDMADE HUGS

55 GIFTABLE CROCHET PATTERNS

Created by Tiffany Brown and Hannah Brown McKay

Daisy Farm Crafts

HANDMADE HUGS

By Daisy Farm Crafts

Created by Tiffany Brown and
Hannah Brown McKay

Paperback ISBN:
979-8-9859326-9-0

Patterns designed and created by
Tiffany Brown
Hannah Brown McKay
Nicolina Brown
Haley Brown
Annie Brown

Extra Photography by
Elizabeth Arnett Brown
Meagan Nolan Wilson

CONTENTS

Introduction / 6

Tips Before Getting Started / 7

Abbreviations & Stitches / 8

Baby Blankets / 10

Throws / 58

Winter Wear / 80

Hot Pads / 112

INTRODUCTION

Hello and welcome to our latest book of crochet patterns!

My daughter Hannah has been working hard converting more of our favorite and most popular patterns from our website into this book, something that I hope you'll be able to enjoy for years to come. We decided to call this book *Handmade Hugs* because gifting crochet sometimes feels like when all else fails, a little bit of handmade goodness can feel just like a hug to someone else.

All of the patterns in this book were designed and created by myself or my four daughters, and if you've been following Daisy Farm Crafts for a while, you'll know that keeping the art of crochet moving through generations is important to me. How I'm choosing to do that is to write our patterns in a more explanatory and approachable way. My hope is that anyone with just the basic crochet knowledge will be able to pick up this book and be successful.

Thank you all for your continued love and support as we've shared what we've been making for friends and family. What started as just a wish to become a grandma by crocheting a few blankets has brought more love and joy into my life than I could ever imagine.

Love,

Tiffany

TIPS BEFORE GETTING STARTED

- When counting chains, never count the loop around the hook.

- There are three ways to work into a base chain: the back loop only, the back loop and underneath the back bump, or into the back bump only. It is personal preference as to which way is chosen.

- It is assumed that a stitch is always worked into the top of the stitch of the previous row unless otherwise stated specifically, such as back loop only or front loop only.

- Stitch markers are extremely helpful for keeping the sides of the work straight. Place a marker in the first stitch of each row. Upon returning, it will be the last stitch to be worked into. The last stitch worked into becomes the first stitch of the next row.

- Turning chains do not count as a stitch unless noted in the instructions. Usually, turning chains provide height to get up to the next row.

- When changing colors or switching to a new skein of yarn, work the stitch until the last step of the stitch (when you still have loops on your hook) and pull through the loops with the new yarn. Unless noted in the pattern, cut the yarn and leave a long tail that you can weave into your project with a tapestry needle.

- If you'd like to add finishing touches to your crochet project, lay it out flat on a towel or foam blocking boards if you have them. Use a spray bottle with water to dampen. Press into straight lines, massaging the stitches and adjusting your tension. Pin with straight pins and let dry.

- All gauge measurements were taken directly from each project.

- Hook sizes specified in patterns are recommendations; if you find that your project is turning out too loose or too tight, don't be afraid to try a different hook size.

- You can find video or stitch tutorials for most of the patterns in this book on the Daisy Farm Crafts YouTube Channel. You'll notice that some of the patterns include a QR code at the bottom of the page; if you'd like you can use the camera app on your phone to scan the code and be taken directly to the video tutorial for that specific pattern. Happy Crocheting!

ABBREVIATIONS & STITCHES

(US TERMS)

Berry Stitch: Yarn over (YO), insert your hook, YO and pull up a loop, YO, pull through one loop, YO, insert your hook into same stitch, YO and pull up a loop, YO, pull through all five loops on hook.

CH: Chain (YO and pull through)

Dot: *YO, insert your hook, YO and pull up a loop. Repeat from * three more times into same stitch. YO and pull through all loops on hook.

Double Crochet (DC): YO, insert your hook, YO and pull up a loop, YO and pull through two loops, YO and pull through remaining two loops on hook.

Double Crochet 2 Together (DC2TOG): YO, insert your hook, YO and pull up a loop, YO, pull through two loops on hook, YO, insert your hook into the next stitch, YO and pull up a loop, YO, pull through two loops, YO, pull through remaining three loops on hook.

Double Crochet 3 Together (DC3TOG): *YO, insert your hook, YO and pull up a loop, YO, pull through two loops on hook. Repeat from * across the next two stitches, then YO and pull through remaining loops on hook.

Double Crochet 5 Together (DC5TOG): *YO, insert your hook, YO and pull up a loop, YO, pull through two loops on hook. Repeat from * across the next four stitches, then YO and pull through remaining loops on hook.

Double Crochet 2 Together Cluster (CL): YO, insert your hook, YO and pull up a loop, YO, pull through two loops on hook. YO, insert hook into same stitch, YO and pull up a loop, YO, pull through two loops, YO, pull through three remaining loops on hook.

Double Crochet 4 Together (DC4TOG) Bobble: *YO, insert your hook, YO and pull up a loop, YO and pull through two loops on hook. Repeat from * 3 more times into same stitch. Then YO and pull through all loops on hook.

Double Crochet 5 Together (DC5TOG) Bobble: *YO, insert your hook, YO and pull up a loop, YO and pull through two loops on hook. Repeat from * 4 more times into same stitch. Then YO and pull through all loops on hook.

Front and Back Post Double Crochet (FPDC & BPDC): A front post DC means you insert your hook from front to back around the post of the next DC and work a DC. A back post DC means you insert your hook from back to front around the post of the next DC and work a DC.

Front Post Treble Crochet (FPTC): YO twice, insert your hook around post (from front to back and back to the front, popping the post forward), YO and pull up a loop, YO, pull through two loops, YO, pull through two loops again, YO, pull through remaining two loops on hook.

Half Double Crochet (HDC): YO, insert your hook, YO and pull up a loop, YO and pull through three loops on hook.

Half Double Slip Stitch (HDSS): YO, insert your hook, YO, pull up a loop and pull directly through two loops on hook.

Half Double Crochet Cluster (HDC-CL): YO, insert your hook, YO and pull up a loop. YO, insert your hook into same stitch, YO and pull up a loop, YO and pull through all five loops on hook.

Half Double Crochet 2 Together (HDC2TOG): YO, insert your hook, YO and pull up a loop. YO, insert your hook into the next stitch, YO and pull up a loop. YO, pull through all five loops on hook.

Herringbone Half Double Crochet (HHDC): YO, insert your hook, YO, pull up a loop and pull directly through first loop on hook. YO and pull through remaining two loops on hook.

Large Puff Stitch: *YO, insert your hook, YO and pull up a loop. Repeat from * three more times, inserting your hook into the same stitch. YO and pull through all loops on hook.

Small Puff Stitch: *YO, insert your hook, YO and pull up a loop. Repeat from * two more times, inserting your hook into the same stitch. Then YO, and pull through all loops on hook.

Single Crochet (SC): Insert your hook, YO and pull up a loop, YO and pull through two loops on hook.

Single Crochet 2 Together (SC2TOG): Insert your hook, YO and pull up a loop, insert your hook into the next stitch, YO and pull up a loop, YO and pull through all three loops on hook.

SK: Skip

Slip Stitch (SL ST): Insert your hook, YO, pull up a loop and pull directly through loop on hook.

ST: Stitch

Treble Crochet (TC): YO twice, insert your hook, YO and pull up a loop, YO and pull through two loops on hook, YO and pull through two loops again, YO and pull through remaining two loops on hook.

Wide Half Double Crochet (WHDC): YO, insert your hook between the stitches (posts) of the previous row, YO and pull up a loop, YO, pull through three loops on hook.

Wide Half Double Crochet Cluster (WHDC-CL): YO, insert your hook between the stitches (posts) of the previous row, YO and pull up a loop, YO, insert hook again into same space, YO and pull up another loop, YO, pull through all loops on hook.

YO: Yarn Over

BABY
BLANKETS

BABY T BLANKET

YARN

Caron Simply Soft
100% acrylic
170 g/6 oz, 288 m/315 yds

COLORS

4 skeins White
1 skein Persimmon
1 skein Light Country Peach
1 skein Light Country Blue
1 skein Country Blue

TOOLS

Size H/5.00mm hook
Tapestry needle
Scissors

SIZE

34 in x 36 in

GAUGE

4 in = 18 st, 18 rows pattern

STITCHES

Single Crochet (SC)

PATTERN

Chain 130 with White. (Pattern repeat is any even number.)

Row 1: Work 1 SC into the 2nd chain from the hook. *CH 1, skip 1 chain, SC into the next chain. Repeat from * across to the end of the chain. The last stitch should be a SC. CH 1 and turn.

Row 2: Work 1 SC into the first SC. *CH 1, skip 1 chain, SC into the next SC. Repeat from * across the row (Mesh stitch). CH 1 and turn.

Rows 3 - 10: Repeat row 2 with White.

Repeat row 2 with following color changes: 2 rows Light Country Blue, 8 rows Country Blue, 4 rows Light Country Peach, 6 rows Persimmon, 10 rows White, 14 rows Light Country Blue, 2 rows Country Blue, 2 rows Light Country Peach, 2 rows Persimmon, 10 rows White, 4 rows Light Country Blue, 4 rows Country Blue, 6 rows Light Country Peach, 6 rows Persimmon, 10 rows White, 4 rows Light Country Blue, 10 rows Country Blue, 2 rows Light Country Peach, 4 rows Persimmon, 10 rows White.

BORDER

With White, pull up a loop in any corner and CH 1. SC into that space. Work 1 SC into each stitch around as evenly as possible. Work 1 SC around the chain 1 spaces as well, and work 3 SC into each corner.

Join with a slip stitch to the starting SC. CH 10. Starting in the 2nd chain from the hook, *work 1 SC. Work 1 SC into the back loop of each of the next 8 chains back toward the edge of the blanket. Slip stitch into the next stitch, and in the next stitch. Turn and work SC in the back loops of each of the 8 SC you just made; work 1 SC into the last stitch (9 SC total). CH 1 and turn. Repeat from * across the edge of the blanket.

In the first of the three stitches that make the corner, only slip stitch once before turning and working the SC back up to the edge of the border. Turn, work back down and slip stitch into the corner space. Turn and work the SC back up to the edge of the border.

When you return to the corner stitch, slip stitch again into the same corner stitch, then work the SC up to the edge. Upon returning, slip stitch one more time into the same corner space for a total of 3 times, before moving on and only slip stitching one time into the next space.

Tip: You may adjust the number of slip stitches in between rows if the edge is stretching or the blanket edge is rippling. You may prefer just doing 1 slip stitch instead of 2.

When all sides are complete, use a tapestry needle to sew the last side to the beginning chain 10. Tie off and weave in the ends.

-Annie

BUNDLE UP DOTS BLANKET

YARN

Bernat Bundle Up
100% polyester
140 g/4.9 oz, 244 m/267 yds

COLORS

5 skeins Posy

TOOLS

Size I/5.50mm hook
Tapestry needle
Scissors

SIZE

35 in x 35 in

GAUGE

4 in = 14 st, 12 rows HDC

STITCHES

Half Double Crochet (HDC)
Single Crochet (SC)
Double Crochet 5 Together
Bobble (Bobble)
Slip Stitch (SL ST)

VIDEO

PATTERN

Chain 120. (Pattern repeat is any multiple of 10.)

Row 1: Starting in the 2nd chain from the hook, work 1 HDC. 1 HDC in each chain to the end of the row. CH 1 and turn. (119)

Rows 2 - 5: Work 1 HDC in each stitch across the row. CH 1 and turn.

Row 6: Work 1 SC into each of the first 9 stitches, *Bobble in the next stitch. Work SC into each of the next 9 stitches. Repeat from * across the row ending with 9 SC to the end of the row. CH 1 and turn.

Repeat rows 2 through 6 for the remainder of the blanket until the height is 35 inches or until your blanket is square. End the blanket with rows 2 - 5.

BORDER

Round 1: After making the very last HDC of the blanket, CH 1 and HDC into the same space as the last HDC. Don't turn; instead rotate the blanket to work down the side. Work approximately 3 HDC per 2 rows on the sides, or as evenly as possible. Work HDC, CH 1, HDC for each corner. Work last HDC into the first chain 1 space of the corner. Don't turn.

Ribbing: CH 8. Work 1 HDC into the 2nd chain from the hook and each chain. *Slip stitch into the next HDC on the edge of the blanket and the next. Work 1 HDC into the back loop of each HDC, CH 1 and turn. Work 1 HDC into the back loop of each HDC and repeat from *.

Tip #1: The ribbing border is worked perpendicular to the blanket.

Tip #2: When approaching the corners, only slip stitch one time over; for the actual corner, work the slip stitch into the same chain 1 space 2 times. Then, on the next pass, only slip stitch one time to the next stitch. You are trying to get the ribbing to fan around the corner.

On the last row of ribbing, tie off and cut yarn with a long tail. Use a tapestry needle to sew the last row to the first row joining the two ends together.

Weave in all ends and tie off.

-Tiffany

VELVET CHANDELIER BABY BLANKET

YARN

Bernat Baby Velvet
100% polyester
3.5 oz/100 g, 149 m/163 yds

COLORS

6 skeins Misty Gray
1 skein each Tiny Teal, Potpourri,
Yolk Yellow, Seafoam, Pink Mist,
Winter White

TOOLS

Size H/5.00mm hook
Tapestry needle
Scissors

SIZE

30 in x 42 in

GAUGE

4 in = 16 st, 14 rows WHDC

STITCHES

Half Double Crochet (HDC)
Wide Half Double Crochet
(WHDC)
Double Crochet (DC)
Front and Back Post Double
Crochet (FPDC & BPDC)

VIDEO

PATTERN

Instructions:

-Lay whichever color you aren't using along the top of your work and crochet over it as you go. To avoid your yarn getting twisted as you carry it along your work, it helps to always keep one color to the front and one color to the back each time you switch colors.

-When turning to a new row, wrap the color not in use around the side of your work and continue to crochet over it as you go.

-To better cover up yarn that is being carried through, always insert your hook underneath the yarn that was carried across the previous row.

Chain 107 with Misty Gray. (Pattern repeat is a multiple of 6, plus 5.)

Row 1: Starting in the 3rd chain from the hook, work 1 HDC into each chain with Misty Gray. CH 2 and turn.

Rows 2 - 3: Work 1 WHDC into each space across the row. CH 2 and turn.

Rows 4 - 11: Work 1 WHDC into each of the first 3 spaces with Misty Gray, then work 1 WHDC into each of the next 3 spaces with Tiny Teal. Continue alternating Misty Gray and Tiny Teal every three stitches. CH 2 and turn. (When you finish row 11, cut the Tiny Teal.)

Rows 12 - 14: With Misty Gray, work 1 WHDC into each space across the row. CH 2 and turn.

Repeat rows 4 through 14 for the remainder of the blanket, switching to a new color each time you repeat rows 4 - 11.

Color changes: 3 rows Misty Gray, *8 rows with Tiny Teal, 3 rows Misty Gray, 8 rows with Potpourri, 3 rows Misty Gray, 8 rows with Yolk Yellow, 3 rows Misty Gray, 8 rows with Seafoam, 3 rows Misty Gray, 8 rows with Pink Mist, 3 rows Misty Gray, 8 rows with Winter White, 3 rows Misty Gray. Repeat from *. Weave in ends.

BORDER

Round 1: With Misty Gray, work 1 DC into each stitch and 1 DC per row on the sides of the blanket. Work 5 DC into each corner space. Join with a slip stitch to the beginning DC. Continue in the same direction.

Round 2: Work alternating FPDC and BPDC around each DC. When you reach a corner, work 3 alternating FPDC and BPDC around the middle DC of the round prior.

Rounds 3 - 4: Continue working in same direction and repeat round 2. Always match your post DCs so they are popping out in same direction as previous row. Slip stitch into starting corner and tie off.

-Hannah

SEA STRIPES BABY BLANKET

YARN

Bernat Forever Fleece
100% polyester
280 g/9.9 oz, 177 m/194 yds

COLORS

2 skeins Balsam
1 skein each Juniper,
Dark Eucalyptus, Sage,
White Noise

TOOLS

Size M/N/9.00mm hook
Tapestry needle
Scissors

SIZE

34 in x 38 in

GAUGE

4 in = 9 st, 8 rows pattern

STITCHES

Single Crochet (SC)
Double Crochet (DC)
Slip Stitch (SL ST)

VIDEO

PATTERN

Chain 66 with Balsam. (Pattern repeat is any even number.)

Row 1: Starting in the 2nd chain from the hook, work 1 SC. *Work 1 DC into the next stitch, then 1 SC into the next stitch. Repeat from * to the end of the row. CH 1 and turn.

Row 2: Work 1 SC into the last SC from previous row. Work 1 DC into next DC, then work 1 SC into next SC. Continue alternating DC and SC across the row. You should always work a DC into the top of a DC and SC into the top of a SC from the row below. CH 1 and turn.

Repeat row 2 for the remainder of the blanket, working the color changes as follows: *4 rows Balsam, 4 rows Juniper, 4 rows Dark Eucalyptus, 4 rows Sage, 4 rows White Noise. Repeat from * 2 more times.

To change colors at the end of a row, stop on your last SC when you still have two loops on your hook, and pull through with the new color. Cut the old color, leaving a long tail you can weave into the blanket later. Then CH 1 with the new color and turn. When you've finished your last row, tie off and weave in all ends before beginning the border.

BORDER

Round 1: Pull up a loop in any corner and CH 1. Work one round of SC around the blanket, working 1 stitch per row on the sides of the blanket and 3 SCs into each corner. When you reach the corner you started with, work your last SC, then slip stitch into the starting stitch.

Round 2: Continuing on in the same direction, CH 4 (or any number if you'd like your border wider). Starting in the 2nd chain from the hook, SC in each of the 3 chains back toward the edge of the blanket. Slip stitch into the next stitch, and in the next stitch. Turn and work in the back loops of each of the 3 SC you just made. CH 1 and turn. Work back down and SC in the back loops only. (Be careful not to miss the 3rd stitch, it sometimes pulls tight and is hard to see.) Repeat around the blanket.

Corners: In the first of the three stitches that make the corner, only slip stitch once, before turning and working the SC back up to the edge. Return and slip stitch into the corner space. Turn and work the SC back up to the edge. When you return to the corner space, slip stitch again into the same corner space, then work the SC up to the edge. Upon returning, slip stitch one more time into the same corner space for a total of 3 times, before moving on and working border as before.

When you reach the corner you started with, tie off at the top of the border, leaving yourself a long tail, then use the tail to sew the sides of the corners together with a tapestry needle.

-Hannah

GOLD PUFFS BABY BLANKET

YARN

Red Heart Super Saver
100% acrylic
198 g/7 oz, 333 m/364 yds

COLORS

4 skeins Saffron

TOOLS

Size I/5.50mm hook
Tapestry needle
Scissors

SIZE

35 in x 38 in

GAUGE

4 in = 16 st, 20 rows pattern

STITCHES

Single Crochet (SC)
Large Puff Stitch
Double Crochet (DC)
Front and Back Post Double
Crochet (FPDC & BPDC)

PATTERN

Chain 120. (Pattern repeat is any even number.)

Row 1: Starting in the 4th chain from the hook, work 1 SC, then CH 1. Skip the next chain then work another SC, CH 1. Continue working SC, CH 1 in every other chain. You should end with one SC in the last chain. CH 2 and turn.

Row 2: Work a SC, CH 1 into the chain one space of the row below. Skip the next stitch, then work a SC, CH 1 in the next chain one space. Continue working SC, CH 1 into the all the chain one spaces from the row below. End with a SC that is between the last stitch and the turning chain of the row below. CH 2 and turn.

Rows 3 - 7: Repeat row 2 (Moss stitch).

Row 8: Repeat row 2, but replace each SC with 1 Large Puff stitch. Work 1 Puff, CH 1 into the all the chain one spaces from the row below, except when you reach the very last space; end with a SC that is between the last stitch and the turning chain of the row below. CH 2 and turn.

Rows 9 - 12: Repeat rows 2 and 8.

Rows 13 - 19: Repeat row 2.

Row 20: Repeat row 8.

Repeat rows 1 through 20 for the remainder of the blanket. Repeat the sequence five more times, ending the blanket with 7 rows of Moss stitch to match the beginning of the blanket. Weave in ends.

BORDER

Round 1: Pull up a loop in any corner and CH 2. Work SC, CH 1 in every other space around the blanket. Work 3 SCs into each corner.

Round 2: Work 3 SCs into starting corner, then keep working in the same direction and work a DC in the top of each stitch around the blanket. Work 3 DCs into each corner.

Round 3: Work 3 DCs into starting corner, then continue in same direction, this time alternating FPDC and BPDC. When you get to the corners of this row, you will want to continue the pattern of alternating FPDC and BPDC, but you will work 3 stitches around the corner post.

Rounds 4 - 6: Work 3 alternating FPDC/BPDC at starting corner and continue alternating FPDC and BPDC around the blanket, working corners in same manner as round 3. Always match your post DCs so that they are poking out in the same direction as the previous row. When finished, slip stitch into the starting corner and tie off.

-Hannah

MINI-CHECKED GINGHAM BLANKET

YARN

Caron Simply Soft
100% acrylic
170 g/6 oz, 288 m/315 yds

COLORS

2 skeins Country Blue
2 skeins Dark Country Blue
1 skein Light Country Blue

TOOLS

Size I/5.50mm hook
Tapestry needle
Scissors

SIZE

30 in x 30 in

GAUGE

4 in = 16 st, 11 rows HHDC

STITCHES

Herringbone Half Double
Crochet (HHDC)
Double Crochet (DC)
Front and Back Post Double
Crochet (FPDC & BPDC)
Single Crochet (SC)

VIDEO

PATTERN

Chain 113 with Country Blue. (Pattern repeat is any odd number multiplied by 3, plus 2.)

Row 1: Starting in the 3rd chain from the hook, work 1 HHDC in each of the next 3 chains. Before finishing the 3rd stitch, pull Dark Country Blue through to change color. Work 3 HHDC in each of the next 3 chains, crocheting over Country Blue and bringing it along the row. Before finishing the 3rd stitch, pull through with Country Blue. Repeat across the row alternating colors every 3 stitches and working over the color not in use. CH 2 and turn.

Row 2: (Wrap Dark Country Blue around the end of the row.) Work the first 3 stitches in Country Blue, working over Dark Country Blue. Change colors every 3 stitches as row 1. In final stitch of the row, pull through with Light Country Blue. CH 2 and turn.

Row 3: With Light Country Blue, work HHDC in each of the first 3 stitches working over Country Blue. Pull through with Country Blue on the 3rd stitch. Alternate colors every 3 stitches as before. CH 2 and turn.

Row 4: (Wrap Country Blue around the end of the row.) Work the first 3 stitches in Light Country Blue working over Country Blue. Change colors every 3 stitches as before. In final stitch of the row, pull through with Country Blue. *Tip: Before starting row 5 with Country Blue, bring Dark Country Blue up the side of the blanket and work the first 3 stitches carrying it along.*

For rest of blanket: Continue alternating colors every 2 rows until blanket is square. I ended on a set of alternating Dark Country Blue and Country Blue to match the first row. Weave in ends.

BORDER

Round 1: With Dark Country Blue, pull up a loop in any corner, CH 2. Work 1 HHDC into the same space. Work 3 HHDC per 2 rows on sides of blanket, and 3 HHDC per 2 stitches on ends of blanket. Work 3 HHDC into each corner. Work 1 HHDC in starting space, join with slip stitch, CH 2 and turn.

Round 2: Work 1 DC into each stitch around, and work 3 DC into each corner stitch. Join with a slip stitch, CH 2 and turn.

Rounds 3 - 5: *Work 1 FPDC around the next DC, BPDC around next DC. Repeat from * around on the sides. On each corner work alternating FPDC and BPDC 3 times around the middle post. Join with a slip stitch at the end of the round, CH 2 and turn.

Final Round: Work 1 SC into each stitch and 3 SC into each corner stitch. Join and tie off. Weave in ends.

-Tiffany

FRUITY STRIPES BABY BLANKET

YARN

Bernat Softee Baby
100% acrylic
140g/5 oz, 331 m/362 yds

COLORS

3 skeins Soft Peach
2 skeins White

TOOLS

Size 4.50mm hook
Tapestry needle
Scissors

SIZE

29 in x 29 in

GAUGE

4 in = 9 st, 17 rows pattern

STITCHES

Single Crochet (SC)
Berry Stitch
Double Crochet (DC)
Front and Back Post Double
Crochet (FPDC & BPDC)

PATTERN

Chain 110 with Soft Peach. (Pattern repeat is any even number.)

Row 1: Starting in the 2nd chain from the hook, work 1 SC. *Berry stitch into the next chain, then SC into the next chain. Repeat from * to the end of the row. CH 1 and turn.

Row 2: Work 1 SC into each stitch across the row. CH 1 and turn.

Row 3: Work 1 SC into the first stitch. *Berry stitch into the next stitch, then SC into the next stitch. Repeat from * to the end of the row. CH 1 and turn.

Rows 4 - 7: Repeat rows 2 and 3.

Row 8: Repeat row 2. On the last stitch of the row, pull through with White just before you finish the SC, when you have two loops on your hook. CH 1 and turn. Cut the Peach and leave a tail you can weave into the blanket later.

Row 9: Repeat row 3.

Rows 10 - 15: Repeat rows 2 and 3.

Row 16: Repeat row 2. On the last stitch of the row, pull through with Peach. CH 1 and turn.

Repeat rows 1 through 16 for the remainder of the blanket. I ended my blanket when I had 8 Peach stripes and 7 White Stripes. End the blanket with a Berry stitch row so that it matches the other end. Weave in ends.

BORDER

Round 1: Pull up a loop in corner and CH 3. Work one round of DC around the blanket, working one DC per row on the sides and one DC per stitch on the ends. Work 3 DCs into each corner.

Round 2: When you reach the corner you started with, work 3 DCs into the corner, then go around the blanket again in the same direction, this time alternating FPDC and BPDC. When you get to the corners of this row, you will want to continue the pattern of alternating FPDC and BPDC, but you will work three stitches around the corner post.

Round 3: When you finish round 2, work 3 alternating FPDC and BPDC into the corner you started with and repeat round 2 around the blanket. Always match your post DCs so that they are poking out in the same direction as the previous row.

Round 4: Repeat round 3. When finished, slip stitch into the starting stitch and tie off.

-Hannah

CHUNKY V-STITCH BLANKET

YARN

Bernat Forever Fleece
100% polyester
280 g/9.9 oz, 177 m/194 yds

COLORS

3 skeins Juniper
1 skein White Noise

TOOLS

Size L/8.00mm hook
Size M/N/9.00mm hook
Tapestry needle
Scissors

SIZE

33 in x 36 in

GAUGE

4 in = 8 st, 7 rows pattern

STITCHES

Double Crochet (DC)

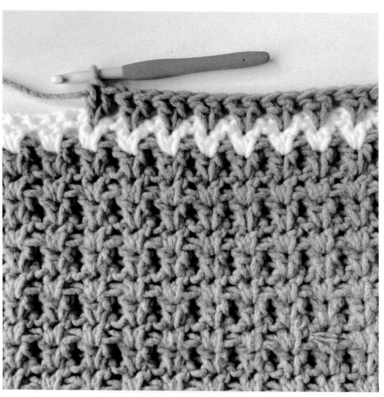

PATTERN

With 9mm hook, **chain 62** with Juniper. (Pattern repeat is any even number.)

Switch to 8mm hook.

Row 1: In the 4th chain from the hook, work 2 DC. Skip the next chain, *2 DC in the next chain, skip the next chain. Repeat from * across the row until 2 chains left. Skip 1 chain, then 1 DC into the very last chain. CH 3 and turn. (This will count as your first DC on next row.)

Row 2: Work 2 DC in the space between the second and third DC posts, splitting the pair to form a "V." *Skip 2 stitches, then work 2 DC in between the next pair of DC from previous row. Repeat from * across row. End row with 1 DC into the top of the turning chain. CH 3 and turn.

Rows 3 - 4: Repeat row 2 with Juniper.

Row 5: Repeat row 2 with White Noise.

Rows 6 - 7: Repeat row 2 with Juniper.

Row 8: Repeat row 2 with White Noise.

Rows 9 - 10: Repeat row 2 with Juniper.

Row 11: Repeat row 2 with White Noise.

Rows 12 - 39: Repeat row 2 with Juniper.

Rows 40 - 46: Repeat rows 5 through 11.

Rows 47 - 50: Repeat row 2 with Juniper. Tie off and weave in ends.

BORDER

Pull up a loop in any corner and CH 3. Turn and work along the side of your blanket and work *2 DC in the first space, then 1 DC in the next space (I worked into the spaces at the end of each row.) Repeat from * down the side of the blanket. Work 3 DCs into the corner.

Across the end of the blanket, *work 2 DC in the first stitch, then skip 1 stitch, and work 3 DC in the next stitch. (I worked into the stitch spaces that lined up with the "Vs" of my blanket.) Repeat from * across the end of the blanket. Continue working around the blanket, working the other side and other end as before. When you reach the starting corner, slip stitch into starting chain and tie off.

-Hannah

RAINBOW MOSS BABY BLANKET

YARN

Assorted Caron Little Crafties
1 package
100% acrylic
20 g/0.7 oz, 58 m/63 yds

Caron Simply Soft
2 skeins White
100% acrylic
170 g/6 oz, 288 m/315 yds

TOOLS

Size H/5.00mm hook
Tapestry needle
Scissors
Stitch Marker

SIZE

27 in x 30 in

GAUGE

4 in = 20 st, 20 rows pattern

STITCHES

Single Crochet (SC)

VIDEO

PATTERN

Chain 126 with White. (Pattern repeat is any even number.)

Row 1: SC in the 4th chain from hook, *CH 1, skip next chain, SC in next chain, repeat from * to the end of the row. On the last SC of the row, pull through with Color. CH 2 and turn.

Rows 2 and 3: SC in first chain 1 space from the previous row, *CH 1, skip 1 stitch, SC in next chain 1 space, repeat from * to the very end, the last SC should be worked into the space between the chain 2 turning chain and SC from the previous row. CH 2 and turn. (Moss Stitch)

Row 4: Work Moss Stitch with White, carrying Color along the row and crocheting over it as your work, then pulling through with Color at the end of the row.

Rows 5 and 6: Work Moss Stitch with Color.

Repeat rows 4 through 6 for the rest of the blanket making the following Color changes after every 8 rows of color: Red, Pink, Orange, Lemon Yellow, Soft Green, Kelly Green, Mint Green, Light Blue, Dark Blue, Light Purple, Dark Purple. Weave in ends.

BORDER

Round 1: With White, begin border by working "SC, CH 1, SC" in the corner (and in each corner.) Work Moss Stitch around. Join with slip stitch to first SC, CH 1 and turn.

Rounds 2 - 6: Work Moss Stitch around. Join with slip stitch and turn for each round.

-Tiffany

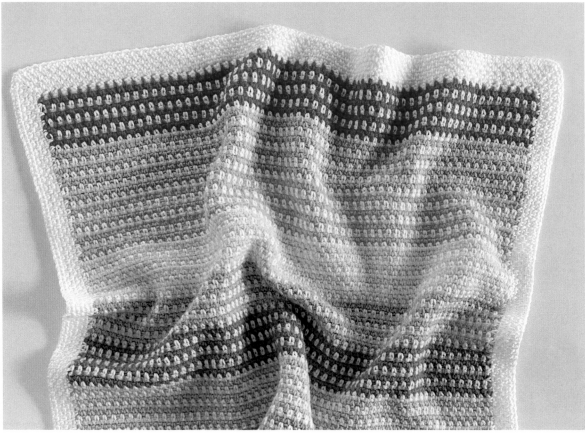

SNOWY MOUNTAINS BABY BLANKET

YARN

Bernat Bundle Up
100% polyester
140 g/4.9 oz, 244 m/267 yds

COLORS

7 skeins Beluga
1 skein Brook
1 skein Cloud White

TOOLS

Size I/5.50mm hook
Tapestry needle
Scissors

SIZE

36 in x 36 in

GAUGE

4 in = 11 st, 14 rows WHDC

STITCHES

Half Double Crochet
Cluster (HDC-CL)
Wide Half Double Crochet
Cluster (WHDC-CL)
Double Crochet (DC)
Front and Back Post Double
Crochet (FPDC & BPDC)

VIDEO

PATTERN

Instructions:

-Pull through with the new color on the last step of the stitch. Lay whichever color you aren't using along the top of your work and crochet over it as you go.

-To avoid your yarn getting twisted as you carry it along your work, it helps to always keep one color to the front and one color to the back each time you switch colors.

-When turning to a new row, wrap the color not in use around the side of your work and continue to crochet over it as you go. To better cover up yarn that is being carried through, always insert your hook underneath the yarn that was carried across the previous row.

Chain 90 with Beluga. (Pattern repeat is a multiple of 16, plus 10.)

Row 1: Starting in the 3rd chain from the hook, work 1 HDC-CL into each chain. CH 2 and turn.

Rows 2 - 8: Work 1 WHDC-CL into each space across the row. (Be sure not to miss the last stitch between the last post and the turning chain.) CH 2 and turn.

Row 9: *Work 1 WHDC-CL in each of the first 8 spaces with Main Color, then work 1 WHDC-CL in each of the next 8 spaces with Brook. Repeat from * across the row. CH 2 and turn.

Rows 10 - 12: Work as row 9, but decrease Brook on each triangle by one stitch on each row. CH 2 and turn.

Rows 13 - 16: Work as rows 10 through 12, but switch triangles to Cloud White, and decrease color on each triangle by one stitch on each row. CH 2 and turn.

Rows 17 - 24: With Main Color, work 1 WHDC-CL in each space across the row. CH 2 and turn.

Row 25: Work 1 WHDC-CL in each of the first 16 spaces with Main Color, then work 1 WHDC-CL in each of the next 8 spaces with Color A. *Work 1 WHDC-CL in each of the next 8 spaces with Beluga, then work 1 WHDC-CL in each of the next 8 spaces with Brook. Repeat from * across the row, until you have 4 triangle bases. End the row with 1 WHDC-CL in each space with Main Color. CH 2 and turn.

Rows 26 - 28: Work as row 25, but decrease Brook on each triangle by one stitch on each row.

Rows 29 - 32: Work as rows 26 - 28, but switch triangles to Cloud White, and decrease color on each triangle by one stitch on each row.

Rows 33 - 40: With Beluga, work 1 WHDC-CL in each space across the row. CH 2 and turn.

Repeat rows 9 through 40 until you have 7 sets of triangles. Weave in ends.

BORDER

Round 1: Pull up a loop in corner and CH 3. Work one round of DC around the blanket, working one DC per row on the sides. On the ends of the blanket, and work *one DC in the first space, then 2 DC in the next space. Repeat from * across each end. Work 5 DCs into each corner.

Round 2: At starting corner, work 5 DCs into corner, then keep working in same direction, this time alternating FPDC and BPDC. At the corners, continue alternating FPDC and BPDC, and work three stitches around the corner post.

Rounds 3 - 5: Work 3 alternating FPDC and BPDC into starting corner, then repeat round 2. Always match your post DCs so they are poking out in the same direction as the row below. When finished, slip stitch into starting stitch and tie off.

-Hannah

BUNDLE UP MODERN DASH BLANKET

YARN

Bernat Bundle Up
100% polyester
140 g/4.9 oz, 244 m/267 yds

COLORS

6 skeins Red Wagon
1 skein Cloud White

TOOLS

Size I/5.50mm hook
Tapestry needle
Scissors

SIZE

33 in x 37 in

GAUGE

4 in = 11 st, 14 rows
WHDC Cluster

STITCHES

Half Double Crochet
Cluster (HDC-CL)
Wide Half Double Crochet
Cluster (WHDC-CL)
Double Crochet (DC)
Front and Back Post Double
Crochet (FPDC & BPDC)

VIDEO

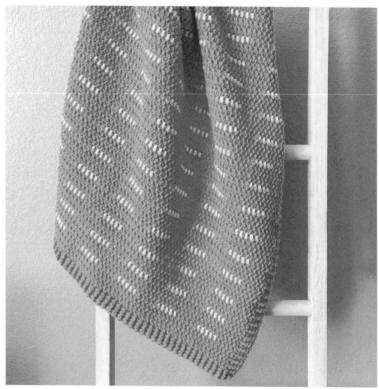

PATTERN

Instructions:

-Pull through with the new color on the last step of the stitch. Lay whichever color you aren't using along the top of your work and crochet over it as you go.

-To avoid your yarn getting twisted as you carry it along your work, it helps to always keep one color to the front and one color to the back each time you switch colors.

-To better cover up yarn that is being carried through, always insert your hook underneath the yarn that was carried across the previous row.

Chain 97 with Red Wagon. (Pattern repeat is 5 multiplied by an odd number, plus 2.)

Row 1: Starting in the 3rd chain from the hook, work 1 HDC-CL into each chain. CH 2 and turn.

Rows 2 - 5: Work 1 WHDC-CL in each space across the row. CH 2 and turn.

Row 6: *Work 1 WHDC-CL in each of the first 5 spaces with Red Wagon, then 1 WHDC-CL in each of the next 5 spaces with Cloud White. Repeat from * to the end of the row. CH 2 and turn.

Rows 7 - 11: With Red Wagon, work 1 WHDC-CL in each space across the row. CH 2 and turn.

Repeat rows 6 through 11 until blanket reaches about 37 inches or desired length. Weave in ends.

BORDER

Round 1: Pull up a loop in any corner and chain 3. Work one round of DC around the blanket, working one DC per row on the sides. On the ends of the blanket, continue inserting your hook in between the posts, and work *one DC in the first space, then 2 DC in the next space. Repeat from * across each end. Work 5 DCs into each corner.

Round 2: At starting corner, work 5 DCs into corner, then keep working in same direction, this time alternating FPDC and BPDC. At the corners, continue alternating FPDC and BPDC, and work three stitches around the corner post.

Rounds 3 - 4: Work 3 alternating FPDC and BPDC into starting corner, then repeat round 2. Always match your post DCs so they are poking out in the same direction as the row below. When finished, slip stitch into starting stitch and tie off.

-Hannah

GRIDDLE STRIPES BABY BLANKET

YARN

Bernat Baby Sport
big ball
100% acrylic
350 g / 12.3 oz,
1148 m / 1256 yds

COLORS

1 skein Baby Grey
1 skein Dark Jade
1 skein Indigo

TOOLS

Size G/4.00mm hook
Tapestry needle
Scissors

SIZE

33 in x 33 in

STITCHES

Single Crochet (SC)
Double Crochet (DC)

PATTERN

Chain 125 with Indigo. (Pattern repeat is any odd number.)

Row 1: Starting in the 2nd chain from hook, work 1 SC. Work 1 DC in the next stitch. *Work 1 SC in the next stitch, then 1 DC in the next stitch. Repeat from * across the row. The last stitch you make should be a DC. CH 1 and turn.

Row 2: Work 1 SC into DC you just made from previous row. Then work 1 DC into the next stitch. *Work 1 SC in the next stitch, then 1 DC in the next stitch. Repeat from * across the row. Always DC into SC. Always SC into DC. CH 1 and turn.

Repeat row 2 for the remainder of the blanket.

Here's how I did my color changes: 6 rows Indigo, *10 rows Baby Grey, 1 row Dark Jade, 3 rows Baby Grey, 6 rows Indigo, 3 rows Baby Grey, 1 row Dark Jade. Repeat from * four times, then end the blanket with 10 rows Baby Grey and 6 rows Indigo.

BORDER

Weave in ends.

Round 1: With Baby Grey, pull up a loop in any corner and CH 1. Work one round of SC around the blanket, working 3 SCs into each corner. When you reach the corner you started with it, slip stitch into the starting stitch, then CH 1 and turn.

Rounds 2 - 4: Work one round of DC, working 3 DCs into each corner. When you reach the corner you started with, slip stitch into the starting stitch, then CH 2 and turn. When you finish the last round, slip stitch into the starting corner and tie off.

-Nicolina

PINK PETAL BABY BLANKET

YARN

Red Heart Soft Baby Steps
100% acrylic
141 g/5 oz, 234 m/256 yds

COLORS

1 skein Soft Pink
3 skeins Strawberry
2 skeins White

TOOLS

Size H/5.00mm hook
Tapestry needle
Scissors

SIZE

30 in x 30 in

STITCHES

Single Crochet (SC)
Slip Stitch (SL ST)
Half Double Crochet (HDC)
Double Crochet 2 Together
Cluster (CL)

VIDEO

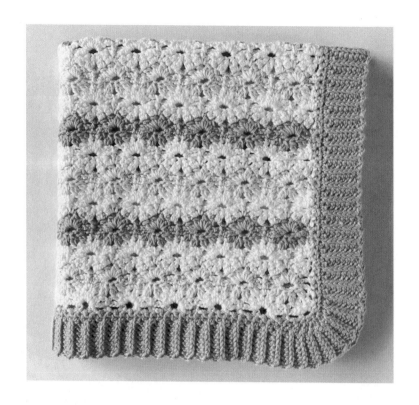

PATTERN

Chain 135 with White. (Pattern repeat is a multiple of 11, plus 3.)

Row 1: In the 2nd chain from the hook, SC, CH 1, skip the next chain, 1 SC into the next chain. *CH 3, skip 3 chains, 1 SC into the next chain. CH 3, skip 3 chains, 1 SC into the next chain. CH 2, skip 2 chains, 1 SC into the next chain.

Repeat from * until 10 chains remain. Then CH 3, skip 3 chains, 1 SC in next chain, CH 3, skip 3 chains, 1 SC in the next chain, CH 1, skip 1 chain, SC in the last chain.

Row 2: CH 3 and turn. In the first chain space, work "CL, CH 2, CL." CH 1, skip the next single crochet and 3 chains, 1 SC into next SC. *CH 1, skip 3 chains and next single crochet. Work 1 CL into chain 2 space. Work "2 CH, CL" 3 times in same chain 2 space (you will have 4 total clusters with 2 chains in between). CH 1. Skip 3 chains, 1 SC into next single crochet, repeat from * to last 7 spaces. CH 1, skip 3 chains, into the last CH 1 space work "CL, CH 2, CL", 1 DC into last SC pulling through with new color.

Row 3: CH 1 and turn. 1 SC into first double crochet, *CH 3, CL into the tops of the next 4 clusters, CH 3, 1 SC into next 2 chain space (the 2 chains that are the middle space between the 4 clusters). Repeat from * to the end, working last SC into top of turning chain.

Row 4: CH 1 and turn. 1 SC into first SC, *CH 3, 1 SC into the top of next cluster, CH 2, skip 2 clusters, 1 SC into top of next cluster, CH 3, skip over 3 chains, 1 SC into next SC. Repeat from * to the end.

Row 5: CH 1 and turn, 1 SC into first SC. *CH 1, skip over 3 chains, 1 CL into next chain 2 space. "CH 2, CL," 3 times in the same chain 2 space. (You will have 4 total clusters with 2 chains in between.) CH 1, skip 3 chains, 1 SC into next SC. Repeat from *to the end, pulling through with new color.

Row 6: CH 3 and turn. 1 CL into each of next two clusters, CH 3, 1 SC in chain 2 space, CH 3. *CL into next four clusters, CH 3, 1 SC into chain 2 space, CH 3, repeat from * to last 2 CL's, work 1 CL into each, 1 DC into last SC.

Row 7: CH 1 and turn, 1 SC into first DC, CH 1, skip the first cluster, 1 SC into next cluster, CH 3, skip 3 chains, 1 SC into next SC, CH 3, *1 SC into next cluster, CH 2, skip 2 clusters, 1 SC into top of next cluster. CH 3, 1 SC into next SC, CH 3, repeat from *to last 2 clusters, 1 SC into next cluster, CH 1, skip 1 cluster, 1 SC into top of turning chain.

Repeat rows 2 - 7 for the rest of the blanket, alternating colors every three rows (after you complete a flower). End the blanket after row 4 instructions so the top matches the starting row. Weave in ends.

BORDER

Round 1: Pull up a loop in corner and work 1 SC. Work 1 SC into each stitch around blanket. Work 3 SC into each corner. At the end of round, SL ST to beginning SC.

Round 2: CH 10. In the 3rd chain from the hook, work 1 HDC. Work 1 HDC into each chain for a total of 8 HDC. SL ST into the top of the next SC on the blanket, and into the next. *Turn the blanket toward you so the row of HDC is facing you. Work 1 front bottom loop HDC (fblHDC) into each of the next 7 stitches. In the last stitch, work under both front loops. CH 2 and turn. Work 1 fblHDC into each of the next 8 stitches. SL ST to the next SC on the blanket and the next. Repeat from * down the first side.

When approaching the 3 SC stitches that make the corner, SL ST once into the first of those single crochets, then turn and work a row of fblHDC. Then turn and work fblHDC back toward the middle SC. SL ST once into the middle SC and then turn and work fblHDC. Upon returning to the middle SC, SL ST into the middle SC one more time. Upon returning to the third SC that makes the corner, SL ST once. Upon returning after working all the corner SC, return to SL ST two times between each row.

Continue repeating the instructions for the sides and corners. Upon returning to the starting row, tie off and weave in ends.

-Tiffany

SQUARED-OFF CHEVRON BLANKET

YARN

Bernat Softee Baby Cotton
60% cotton, 40% acrylic
120 g/4.2 oz, 232 m/254 yds

COLORS

4 skeins Dusk Sky
2 skeins Clear White
2 skeins Feather Gray

TOOLS

Size G/4.00mm hook
Tapestry needle
Scissors

SIZE

34 in x 34 in

GAUGE

2 in = 9 st, 8 rows SC

STITCHES

Single Crochet (SC)
Single Crochet 2 Together
(SC2TOG)
Half Double Crochet (HDC)

VIDEO

PATTERN

Chain 156 with Dusk Sky. (Pattern repeat is a multiple of 31, plus 1.)

Row 1: Begin in the 2nd chain from the hook. SC2TOG, *SC in each of the next 13 chains, 3 SC in next chain, SC in each of the next 13 chains, SC2TOG twice, repeat from * across the row ending with SC2TOG across final 2 chains. CH 1 and turn.

From now on, work in back loops only.

Row 2: SC2TOG first 2 sts, SC in each of the next 13 sts, 3 SC in next st, SC in each of the next 13 sts, SC2TOG twice, repeat from * across the row ending with SC2TOG across final 2 sts. CH 1 and turn.

Tip: SC2TOG twice means that you single crochet across 2 stitches, complete the stitch, then single crochet across the next 2 stitches. You are turning 4 stitches into 2 stitches.

Repeat row 2 instructions until you have the height you want making color changes as follows: *8 rows of blue, 2 rows of white, 2 rows of tan, 2 rows of white, repeat from * and end with 8 rows of blue.

Squaring off the first corner: Change to white at the end of the last row of blue, CH 1 and turn. SC2TOG first 2 stitches, SC in each of the next 14 sts, CH 1 and turn.

Begin in the 2nd stitch, (skip first SC), SC in each of the next 12 sts, SC2TOG last 2 sts, pull through with tan, CH 1 and turn.

SC2TOG, SC in each of the next 11 sts, CH 1 and turn.

Begin in the 2nd st, SC in each of the next 9 sts, SC2TOG last 2 sts, pull through with white, CH 1 and turn.

SC2TOG, SC in each of the next 8 sts, CH 1 and turn.

Begin in the 2nd st, SC in each of the next 6 sts, SC2TOG last 2 sts, pull through with blue, CH 1 and turn.

SC2TOG, SC in each of the next 5 sts, CH 1 and turn.

Begin in the 2nd st, SC in each of the next 3 sts, SC2TOG last 2 sts, CH 1 and turn.

SC2TOG, SC in each of the next 2 sts, CH 1 and turn.

Skip first st, SC2TOG final 2 sts. Tie off.

Filling the valley: With white, pull up a loop in the st in the top of the peak, CH 1 and SC in that st. SK the next st, SC in each of the next 12 sts, SC2TOG twice, SC in each of the next 12 sts, SK one st, SC in next, CH 1 and turn.

Begin in the 2nd st, (skipping the first), SC in each of the next 11 sts, SC2TOG twice, SC in each of the next 11 SC, pull through with tan, CH 1 and turn.

Begin in the 2nd st, SC in each of the next 9 sts, SC2TOG twice, SC in each of the next 9 sts, CH 1 and turn.

Begin in the 2nd st, SC in each of the next 7 sts, SC2TOG twice, SC in each of the next 7 sts, pull through with white, CH 1 and turn.

Begin in the 2nd st, SC in each of the next 5 sts, SC2TOG twice, SC in each of the next 5 sts, CH 1 and turn.

Begin in the 2nd st, SC in each of the next 3 sts, SC2TOG twice, SC in each of the next 3 sts, pull through with blue, CH 1 and turn.

Begin in the 2nd st, SC in the next st, SC2TOG twice, SC in the next st, CH 1 and turn.

SC2TOG, SL ST to the next st, tie off.

Squaring off the second corner: With white, pull up a loop in the top of the peak, CH 1 and SC in that st. SC in each of the next 12 sts, SC2TOG last 2 sts, CH 1 and turn.

SC2TOG first 2 sts, SC in each of next 11 sts, pull through with tan, CH 1 and turn.

Begin in 2nd st, SC in each of the next 9 sts, SC2TOG, CH 1 and turn.

SC2TOG, SC in each of the next 8 SC, pull through with white, CH 1 and turn.

Begin in 2nd st, SC in each of the next 6 SC, SC2TOG, CH 1 and turn.

SC2TOG, SC in each of the next 5 sts, pull through with blue, CH 1 and turn.

Begin in the 2nd st, SC in each of the next 3 sts, SC2TOG, CH 1 and turn.

SC2TOG, SC in next 2 sts, CH 1 and turn.

Begin in the 2nd st, SC2TOG, tie off.

Fill the valleys on the bottom of the blanket by pulling up your first loop in the starting chain corner.

Follow the instructions for "Filling the valley" above with the exception that the SC2TOG are worked across 3 sts instead of 4.

The middle "legs" of the stitch share the same st on the first row where you are working on the underside of the starting chain.

The rest of the instructions for filling in the valley are the same as above. The only exception is on the first row.

BORDER

With blue, work 2 SC at the end of each row, skip a row. Work 3 SC into each corner. Join with a slip stitch to the first st and CH 1. Continue in the same direction working 1 HDC into each SC and 3 HDC into each corner st. Do not join, continue in the same direction with 1 round of SC, working the SC in between each HDC and 3 into each corner st. Don't join, continue in same direction with working 1 SC into each SC and 3 SC into each corner, slip stitch at the end of the second round of SC and tie off.

-Tiffany

BOHO MODERN GRANNY BLANKET

YARN

Caron Simply Soft
100% acrylic
170 g/6 oz, 288 m/315 yds

COLORS

1 skein each White, Plum
Wine, Light Country Peach,
Soft Pink, Pumpkin

TOOLS

Size H/5.00mm hook
Tapestry needle
Scissors

SIZE

36 in x 30 in

GAUGE

4 in = 17 st, 8 rows DC

STITCHES

Single Crochet (SC)
Double Crochet (DC)
Double Crochet 3 Together
(DC3TOG)
Double Crochet 5 Together
(DC5TOG)
Slip Stitch (SL ST)
DC5TOG Bobble

VIDEO

PATTERN

Chain 139 with Plum Wine. (Pattern repeat is a multiple of 3, plus 1.)

Row 1: 1 DC into 4th CH from hook, *SK next 2 CHs, 3 DC into next CH, repeat * ending with 2 DC into last CH, turn.

Row 2: CH 3, 1 DC into next DC, (CH 3 counts as first DC), *CH 2, DC3TOG, repeat from * ending with CH 2, DC into next DC, DC into top of turning chain, pulling through with new color just before you finish the DC.

Row 3: CH 3, 3 DC in the CH 2 space between the last DC3TOG and 2 DC of the previous row, *3 DC into next CH 2 space, repeat from * ending with 1 DC in top of the turning chain.

Row 4: CH 4, (counts as 1 DC and 1 CH), *DC3TOG in top of each 3 DC of previous row, CH 2, repeat from * across and end with CH 1, DC into top of turning chain, pulling through with new color.

Row 5: CH 3, 1 DC into DC (the base of the CH 3, the top of the last DC you made), *3 DC in next CH 2 space, repeat from * across ending with 2 DC into the top of 3rd chain of the turning chain.

Row 6: CH 3, 1 DC into the next DC, *CH 2, DC3TOG, repeat from * ending with CH 2, DC into next DC, DC into 3rd of chain 3 pulling through with new color just before you finish the stitch.

Here are the color changes: 6 rows Plum Wine, 6 rows White, 6 rows Light Country Peach, 6 rows Soft Pink, 6 rows Pumpkin, 6 rows Soft Pink, 6 rows Light Country Peach, 6 rows White, 6 rows Plum Wine. Weave in ends.

BORDER

Round 1: With White, start in a bottom right-hand corner that will have you work up one side. Pull up a loop and SC in that space (around a DC post actually). Work 2 SC around each DC post running up the side of the blanket. Try and do this as evenly as possible. CH 1 and turn.

Round 2: SC in the first chain space, *CH 3, SK two spaces, SC in the next. Repeat from * to the end of the row. (It's totally okay that when you get to the end of the row you might only skip over one space or have an extra at the very last.)

Round 3: CH 1 and turn. SL ST into the CH 3 space. *CH 5, DC5TOG Bobble in the 4th chain from the hook, DC5TOG Bobble in the 5th chain from the hook. SL ST the posts together. SL ST into the same CH 3 space, SL ST into the next CH space. Repeat from * around. Tie off and weave in the ends.

-Tiffany

TULIP RIPPLE BABY BLANKET

YARN

Bernat Bundle Up
100% polyester
140 g/4.9 oz, 244 m/267 yds

COLORS

2 skeins Cloud White
1 skein Brook
1 skein Posy
1 skein Red Wagon

TOOLS

Size I/5.50mm hook
Tapestry needle
Scissors

SIZE

26 in x 26 in

GAUGE

4 in = 14 st, 12 rows pattern

STITCHES

Single Crochet (SC)
Half Double Crochet (HDC)
Double Crochet (DC)
HDC Cluster (HDC-CL)
HDC 2 Together (HDC2TOG)

VIDEO

PATTERN

Chain 111 in Cloud White. (Pattern repeat is a multiple of 36, plus 3.)

Row 1: In the 4th chain from the hook, work 1 DC. *HDC in each of the next 6 chains. HDC2TOG across the next 2 chains and then across the next 2 chains. HDC in each of the next 6 chains. Work 2 DC into the next chain and also 2 DC into the next. Repeat from * until there is 1 chain left. Work 2 DC into the final chain, CH 3 and turn.

Row 2: Work 1 DC into the first DC of the row, (right at the base of the turning chain, not the next one), *HDC into each of the next 6 stitches. HDC2TOG across the next 2 stitches, and then again across the next 2 stitches. HDC in each of the next 6 stitches. Work 2 DC into the next st and also 2 DC into the next st. Repeat from * across the row. Work 2 DC into the top of the turning chain, CH 3 and turn.

Rows 3 - 6: Repeat row 2. (Pull through with Brook on the last step of the stitch of row 6.)

Tip: I did not cut Cloud White, I carried it up the side of the work. I did cut the colors and wove them in after.

Row 7: Work row 2 instructions with Brook. Pull through on the last step of the stitch with Posy.

Row 8: Work 1 DC in the first DC, *HDC-CL in each of the next 6 stitches. HDC2TOG across the next 2 stitches, and then again across the next 2 stitches. HDC-CL in each of the next 6 stitches. Work 2 DC into the next st and also 2 DC into the next st. Repeat from * across the row. Work 2 DC into the top of the turning chain, CH 3 and turn.

Repeat rows 2 through 8 for the remainder of the blanket to the size you desire and ending with 6 rows of Cloud White. I alternated the colors for row 8 between Posy and Red Wagon.

BORDER

Before beginning the border, weave in the ends, then work 2 rounds of SC, working evenly on the sides and 3 SC into each corner. Then join with a slip stitch and tie off.

-Tiffany

VINTAGE FRINGE STRIPES BLANKET

YARN

Caron One Pound
100% acrylic
454g/16 oz, 742 m/812 yds

COLORS

1 skein Golden Dorado
1 skein Off White
1 skein Pale Green

TOOLS

Size H/5.00mm hook
Tapestry needle
Scissors

SIZE

32 in x 36 in

STITCHES

Herringbone Half Double
Crochet (HHDC)
Single Crochet (SC)

VIDEO

PATTERN

Chain 104 with Golden Dorado.

Row 1: Starting in the 3rd chain from the hook, work 1 HHDC into each chain. CH 2 and turn.

Row 2: Work 1 HHDC in the front loop of each stitch across the row. CH 2 and turn.

Repeat row 2 for the remainder of the blanket with the following color changes: 4 rows of Golden Dorado, 4 rows of Off White, 1 row of Pale Green, 4 rows of Off White, 2 rows of Golden Dorado, 1 row of Off White, 2 rows of Golden Dorado, 6 rows of Off White, 2 rows of Pale Green, 6 rows of Off White, 4 rows of Golden Dorado, 2 rows of Off White. Repeat in reverse (4 rows of Golden Dorado, 6 rows of Off White etc..) Weave in ends.

BORDER

Round 1: With White, pull up a loop in corner and CH 1. Work one round of SC around the blanket, working 3 SCs into each corner. Slip stitch into starting stitch, CH 1 and turn.

Rounds 2 - 3: Work one round of front loop HHDC, working 3 HHDCs into each corner. At starting corner, slip stitch into starting stitch, CH 1 and turn. After last round, slip stitch into starting corner and tie off.

To add tassels, use measuring tape to cut several 9 to 10 inch pieces. Take two to three pieces of yarn and fold them in half. Insert the folded end into the chain space above your border row. Pull the ends through the loop and pull tight to make a knot.

-Nicolina

FLOWER BABY BLANKET

YARN

Bernat Softee Cotton
60% cotton, 40% acrylic
120 g/4.2 oz, 232 m/254 yds

COLORS

4 skeins Cotton
1 skein Sandstone

TOOLS

Size G/4.00mm hook
Tapestry needle
Scissors

SIZE

36 in x 36 in

STITCHES

Double Crochet (DC)

PATTERN

Chain 156 with Cotton. (Pattern repeat is any multiple of 3.)

Row 1: Work 1 DC into the 3rd chain from the hook. CH 3. Work the first leg of a DC5TOG into the first chain of chain 3, (YO, insert your hook, YO and pull a loop back through, YO and pull through 2 loops.)

YO and insert your hook into the base of the DC to work the 2nd and 3rd legs of the DC5TOG, (*YO, insert your hook into the base of the DC, YO and pull a loop back through, YO and pull through two loops, repeat from *). Skip 2 chains, YO and insert your hook into the next chain to work the 4th and 5th legs of the DC5TOG (work legs as explained for 3rd and 4th). After making the 5th leg, there should be 6 loops on your hook, YO and pull through all 6 loops.

*CH 3. (The first chain is considered the eye of the flower or center.) Work the first leg of the DC5TOG in the eye, or first chain, work the 2nd and 3rd legs of the DC5TOG in the chain stitch where the last stitch was worked, skip 2 chains, work the 4th and 5th legs into the next chain. Repeat from * across the row. After pulling through all 6 loops at the end of the row, CH 3, work 1 DC into the eye, CH 3, and turn.

Row 2: YO and insert your hook into the first chain, YO and pull through 2 loops, YO and insert your hook into the eye that is directly below the DC and CH 3, work 2nd and 3rd legs, YO and insert your hook into the next eye, work 4th and 5th legs, YO and pull through all 6 loops. *CH 3, YO and work 1st leg in first chain or eye, work 2nd and 3rd leg into next eye, work 4th and 5th into next eye, YO and pull through all 6 loops. Repeat from * across the row. Turn as instructed in row 1 (CH 3, DC, CH 3).

Repeat row 2 instructions until blanket is 30 inches high. Tie off and weave in ends.

BORDER

With Sandstone, pull up a loop in any corner, CH 3. Work 4 DC into the same corner. *Skip 2 stitches, work 1 SC into the next. Skip 2 stitches, work 5 DC into the next. Continue around the entire blanket repeating from *.

Tip: for the sides of the blanket, I estimated where to insert my hook and looked for the "eyes" on the side to help guide me.

Join with a slip stitch to first stitch, tie off.

-Tiffany

VELVET FLOWER ROWS BLANKET

YARN

Bernat Baby Velvet
100% polyester
300 g/10.5 oz, 450 m/492 yds

COLORS

2 skeins Misty Gray
1 skein Snowy White

TOOLS

Size 4.50mm hook
Tapestry needle
Scissors

SIZE

31 in x 31 in

GAUGE

4 in = 15 st, 15 rows WHDC

STITCHES

Half Double Crochet (HDC)
Wide Half Double Crochet
(WHDC)
Large Puff Stitch
Double Crochet (DC)
Front and Back Post Double
Crochet (FPDC & BPDC)

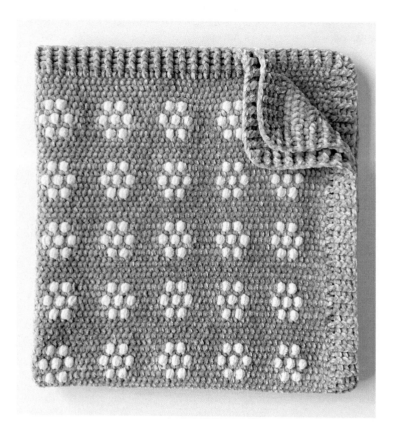

PATTERN

Instructions:

-Pull through with the new color just before you finish the stitch.

-On the flower rows, lay whichever color you aren't using along the top of your work and crochet over it as you go.

-To avoid your yarn getting twisted as you carry it along your work, it helps to always keep one color to the front and one color to the back each time you switch colors.

Chain 107 with Misty Gray. (Pattern repeat is a multiple of 10, plus 7.)

Row 1: Starting in the 3rd chain from the hook, work 1 HDC in each chain. CH 2 and turn.

Rows 2 - 5: Work 1 WHDC in each space across the row. (Make sure not to miss the last space, between the last stitch and the turning chain.) CH 2 and turn. (4 rows)

Row 6: Work 1 WHDC in each of the first 6 spaces with Gray, then work 1 Large Puff stitch with White in the next space, 1 WHDC with Gray in the next space, 1 Puff stitch with White in the next space. *Work 1 WHDC in each of the next 7 spaces with Gray, then 1 Puff stitch with White in the next space, 1 WHDC with Gray in the next space, 1 Puff stitch with White in the next space. Repeat from * to the end of the row, always laying whichever yarn you aren't using across the top of your work and crocheting over it as you go. End the row with WHDC in the last 6 spaces with Gray. CH 2 and turn.

Row 7: Wrap the White around the side of your work and crochet over it as you work 1 WHDC in each space across the row with Gray. CH 2 and turn.

Row 8: Continue crocheting over the White, and *work 1 WHDC in each of the next 5 spaces with Gray, then 1 Puff stitch with White in the next space, 1 WHDC with Gray in the next space, 1 Puff stitch with White in the next space, 1 WHDC with Gray in the next space, 1 Puff stitch with White in the next space. Repeat from * to the end of the row. End the row with WHDC in the last 5 spaces with Gray. CH 2 and turn.

Row 9: Wrap the White around the side of your work and crochet over it as you work 1 WHDC in each space across the row with Gray. CH 2 and turn.

Row 10: Repeat row 6. At the end of the row, cut the White yarn and leave a tail long enough to weave into the blanket later.

Rows 11 - 15: With Gray, work 1 WHDC in each space across the row. CH 2 and turn. (5 rows)

Repeat rows 6 through 15 nine more times, or until you reach your desired length. I ended up with 10 sets of flowers when my blanket was the length I wanted. Weave in ends.

BORDER

Round 1: Pull up a loop in any corner and CH 3. DC around the entire blanket, working 5 DCs into each corner space. Work one DC per stitch on the ends and one DC per row on the sides of the blanket.

Round 2: At starting corner, work 5 DCs into corner, then keep working in same direction, this time alternating FPDC and BPDC. At the corners, continue alternating FPDC and BPDC, and work three stitches around the corner post.

Rounds 3 - 5: Work 3 alternating FPDC and BPDC into starting corner, then repeat round 2. Always match your post DCs so they are poking out in the same direction as the row below. When finished, slip stitch into starting stitch and tie off.

-Hannah

WINDOWPANE PUFF BABY BLANKET

YARN

Patons Beehive Baby Sport
70% acrylic, 30% nylon
100 g/3.5 oz, 328 m/359 yds

COLORS

4 skeins White

TOOLS

Size G/4.00mm hook
Tapestry needle
Scissors

SIZE

32 in x 30 in

STITCHES

Single Crochet (SC)
Small Puff Stitch

VIDEO

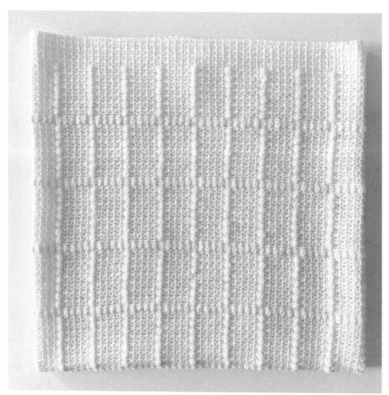

PATTERN

Chain 100. (Pattern repeat is any multiple of 10.)

Tip: Work a small practice swatch and see if using a hook one size smaller for the chain and first row only will help to keep the starting row a bit tighter. The skipped chain on the starting chain can sag and you want to try and avoid that.

Row 1: Work 1 SC into the 2nd chain from the hook. *CH 1 and skip the next chain. Work 1 SC into the next chain space. Repeat from * across the row. You should end with a SC into the last chain. CH 1 and turn. (This is the Mesh stitch.)

Row 2: Work 1 SC into the SC, *CH 1, skip chain, work SC into the SC. Repeat from * 3 times for a total of 5 SC stitches and 4 chain stitches. Work 1 Small Puff around the chain space (the tenth stitch). **Work Mesh stitch across next 9 stitches, work 1 Puff into the 10th chain. Repeat from ** across the row, end with Mesh stitch across the last 9 stitches. CH 1 and turn.

Rows 3 - 15: Repeat rows 1 and 2.

Row 16: *Work SC into SC and Puff stitch around each ch 1. Repeat from * across the row. CH 1 and turn.

Repeat rows 2 - 16 until blanket measures 30 inches or to desired height. Weave in ends.

BORDER

Pull up a loop in any corner, work one round of SC evenly around the entire blanket, working 3 SC into each corner space. (It may help to use one size smaller hook for this round and work 2 SC into the tops of the SCs and skip the CH 1 spaces.) On the sides of the blanket, work 2 SC at the end of a row and then skip a row.

Join with a slip stitch to the end of the round, CH 1 and turn. Change back to the larger hook size if you worked the first round with a smaller hook. Work the Mesh stitch around the blanket, working 3 SC into the middle SC of the corners.

Tip: When approaching the corners, break from the Mesh stitch pattern in order to work 3 SC into the middle stitch. You will always work 3 SC into the middle SC that makes the corner, so if that means 4 SC are in a row, it's okay.

Also, as the rounds grow around the corners, sometimes you will be working a CH across a SC in order to keep the Mesh stitch consistent. Join each round with a slip stitch, CH 1 and turn. Make as many rounds as needed to achieve a 2 inch border (I worked 12 rounds). Tie off and weave in ends.

-Tiffany

BETTYANN'S SWEATER BLANKET

YARN

Red Heart Soft
100% acrylic
141 g/5 oz, 234 m/256 yds

COLORS

4 skeins White
3 skeins Black

TOOLS

Size I/5.50mm hook
Size J/6.00mm hook
Size K/6.50mm hook
Tapestry needle
Scissors

SIZE

36 in x 36 in

GAUGE

4 in = 14 st, 12 rows pattern

STITCHES

Single Crochet (SC)
Double Crochet (DC)
Half Double Crochet (HDC)

VIDEO

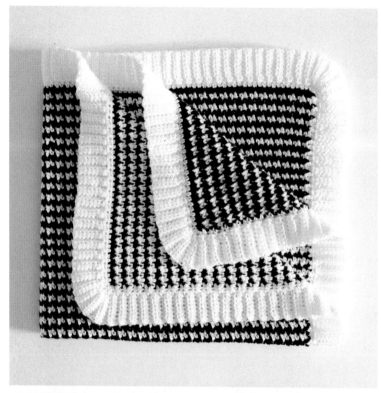

PATTERN

With 6.00mm hook, **chain 111** with Black. (Pattern repeat is any odd number.)

Row 1: In the 2nd chain from hook, *work 1 SC. In the next chain, work 1 DC. Alternate from * in each chain space. The last stitch you make should be a DC. Pull through with White on last stitch. CH 1 and turn.

Switch to 6.5mm hook.

Row 2: With White, work as row 1, carrying the Black along the row with you and crocheting over it. (Note, SCs will work into the tops of the DCs, and DCs into the tops of SCs.) Pull through with Black on the last stitch. CH 1 and turn.

Repeat rows 1 - 2 until blanket measures approximately 34 inches. End with one row of Black. Tie off and weave in ends.

BORDER

With White, pull up a loop in any corner and CH 1. Work 1 HDC into each stitch, work 3 HDC into the corner spaces, and work 1 HDC per row. Join with a slip stitch at the end of the row to the first HDC.

Switch to 5.5mm hook.

Working in the same direction, CH 9. In the 3rd chain from the hook, work HDC and then work HDC into each chain for a total of 7 HDC. Slip stitch into the next stitch that is on the border and the next stitch, turn, skip over the slip stitches and work 7 HDC into the back loops of the HDC you just made down the chain. CH 2 and turn. Work 7 back loop only HDC back down to the edge of the blanket, slip stitch into the next two spaces. Repeat in this manner down the side of the blanket.

When you reach the corner, instead of slip stitching over two times, slip stitch into the corner space three times in a row. Meaning, after you work up and down the HDC's, slip stitch back into the same corner space, repeating three times. This will fan the work around the corner. Then you will return to slip stitching over the next two spaces.

When you have gone all the way around the blanket, finish the last corner by slip stitching 3 times into the same space, then end on the outside edge of the blanket. Tie off leaving a long tail. Sew the last edge to the first edge of the border. Then weave in all remaining ends.

Note: Hook sizes are suggestions; use whichever hook is necessary to obtain gauge.

-Tiffany

BLACK AND WHITE GINGHAM

YARN

Patons Canadiana
100% acrylic
100 g/3.5 oz, 187 m/205 yds

COLORS

5 skeins Pale Gray Mix
2 skeins Black
2 skeins Aran

TOOLS

Size H/5.00mm
Size G/4.00mm
Tapestry needle
Scissors

SIZE

32 in x 30 in

GAUGE

4 in = 17 st, 12 rows HDC

STITCHES

Half Double Crochet (HDC)
Double Crochet (DC)
Front and Back Post Double
Crochet (FPDC & BPDC)

PATTERN

Chain 116 in Black. (Pattern repeat is any odd number multiplied by 6, plus 2.)

Row 1: HDC in the 3rd chain from the hook. HDC in each of the next 5 chains, joining the Pale Gray Mix on the 6th HDC (6 HDC made in Black). HDC with Pale Gray Mix in each of the next 6 chains, crocheting over the Black tail and bringing it along with you laying it flat against the chain. Pull through with Black on the 6th HDC. Alternate across the row switching between Black and Pale Gray Mix every 6 chains. (Always pull through on the last step of the 6th stitch of each color change and always crochet over whichever color you aren't using and carry it along the top of your work.) CH 2 and turn. (Your last color block should be Black.)

Rows 2 - 4: Bringing the Pale Gray Mix around the end of the row, continue crocheting over the tail and HDC in each of the next 6 stitches, then pull through with Pale Gray Mix. Alternate the colors every 6 stitches as in row 1. Always CH 2 and turn.

Rows 5 - 8: At the end of row 4, pull through with Pale Gray Mix and leave off the black. (You may choose here to cut and weave the tail in later, or leave attached and carry the yarn up the side. The border will not completely cover the carried yarn up the side, so if that bothers you, it's better if you cut the yarn and weave it in later.) HDC in each of the first 6 stitches, joining the Aran (cream color) on the 6th stitch. HDC with Aran into each of the next 6 stitches, working over the Pale Gray Mix. Continue the row alternating every six stitches and laying the yarn not being used across the row and working over it. CH 2 and turn.

For the rest of the blanket, continue alternating colors every 4 rows. You will use the Pale Gray Mix in the entire blanket; the Black and Aran can be cut after using them for 4 rows, or you may choose to carry up the side.

BORDER

Round 1: Pull up a loop in any corner and CH 1. HDC into each stitch and HDC 3 times into each corner space. On the sides of the blanket work 6 HDC per 4 rows of color. (If it seems that this is fanning the sides of your blanket too much, try switching to a smaller hook size for the sides.)

Round 2: (If you needed to switch to a smaller hook for the first round, switch back to the hook you used to make the blanket.) Continuing in the same direction, CH 2 and work DC into each stitch around, working 3 DC into the corner stitch (middle of the 3 HDC of the row below). Do not join and do not turn when round is complete.

Rounds 3 - 5: *Work FPDC around each of the next 2 DC, Work BPDC around each of the next 2 DC. Repeat from * to the corner DC. Work 3 regular DC into the corner stitch (middle DC from the row below). Then continue repeating from *. If the pairs of FPDC or BPDC end up uneven before you reach the corner DC, it's okay; you'll pick up the extra FPDC or BPDC on the next round. Tie off and weave in ends at end of round 5.

-Tiffany

THROWS

HERRINGBONE HALF THROW

YARN

Patons Alpaca Blend
60% acrylic, 22% wool
10% nylon, 8% alpaca
100g/3.5oz, 142 m/155 yds

COLORS

8 skeins Birch
1 skein Slate
1 skein Butternut

HOOK

Size J/6.00mm hook

TOOLS

Tapestry needle
Scissors

SIZE

36 in x 60 in

GAUGE

4 in = 15 st, 8 rows HHDC

STITCHES

Herringbone Half Double
Crochet (HHDC)

VIDEO

PATTERN

Chain 92 with Birch.

Row 1: Starting in the 3rd chain from the hook, work 1 HHDC in each chain. CH 2 and turn. (90 st)

Row 2: Work 1 HHDC in the front loop of each stitch across the row. CH 2 and turn.

Repeat row 2 with following color changes: *10 rows Birch, 1 row Slate, 3 rows Birch, 1 row Slate, 3 rows Birch, 1 row Slate, 3 rows Birch, 1 row Slate, 10 rows Birch, 1 row Butternut, 3 rows Birch, 1 row Butternut, 3 rows Birch, 1 row Butternut, 3 rows Birch, 1 row Butternut.

Repeat from * two more times, and end the blanket with 10 rows Birch. Weave in ends.

BORDER

Pull up a loop in any corner and CH 2. Work 1 HHDC per stitch around the entire blanket, working 3 HHDC into each corner space. When returning to the starting corner, work 2 HHDC and slip stitch to starting chain. CH 2 and turn.

Work the next round in the same manner, into the front loops of each stitch as you did the main blanket. Always work 3 HHDC into each corner. Work the border for a total of 5 rounds. Slip stitch into final space, then tie off and weave in ends.

-Tiffany

FOREVER FLEECE THROW

YARN

Bernat Forever Fleece
100% polyester
280 g/9.9 oz, 177 m/194 yds

COLORS

6 skeins Dark Eucalyptus

HOOK

Size M/N/9.00mm hook

TOOLS

Tapestry needle
Scissors

SIZE

Finished size 50 in x 37 in

GAUGE

4 in = 9 st, 8 rows pattern

STITCHES

Single Crochet (SC)

PATTERN

Chain 121. (Pattern repeat is any odd number.)

Row 1: Starting in the 2nd chain from the hook, work 1 SC. 1 SC into each chain across, CH 1 and turn. (120 st)

Row 2: Work 1 SC into the first SC. 1 front loop SC into each of the next 118 stitches. Work 1 SC into last SC.

Tip: Working the first and last SC of the row under the top two loops like usual will help when you attach the tassels, the rest of the single crochets are worked into the front loops.

Rows 3 - 4: Repeat row 2.

Rows 5 - 6: Work 1 SC into the first SC. *Skip the next SC, work front loop SC into the next, work front loop SC into the skipped stitch. Repeat from * across to the last stitch, work 1 SC into the final SC. CH 1 and turn.

For the rest of the blanket repeat the sequence of 4 rows of front loop SC, then 2 rows of the skipped SC rows 8 times, then end with 4 rows of front loop SC.

Tip: Avoid changing yarn mid row. When you are approaching the end of a skein, it's best with this yarn to make the switch to the next skein at the end of a row.

Tie off and weave in the ends. I also knotted the yarn together at the ends of the blanket where the yarn changes occurred for extra security.

Attach tassels by cutting 14 inch pieces. I used 4 pieces per tassel.

-Tiffany

VELVET BUFFALO CHECK THROW

YARN

Bernat Velvet
100% polyester
300 g/10.5 oz, 288 m/315 yds

COLORS

3 skeins Black
2 skeins Misty Gray
2 skeins Vapor Gray
2 skeins White

TOOLS

Size J/6.00mm hook
Tapestry needle
Scissors

SIZE

40 in x 60 in

GAUGE

4 in = 12 st, 12 rows WHDC

STITCHES

Half Double Crochet (HDC)
Wide Half Double Crochet
(WHDC)
Double Crochet (DC)
Front and Back Post Double
Crochet (FPDC & BPDC)

VIDEO

PATTERN

Chain 110 with Vapor Gray. (Pattern repeat is an odd number multiplied by 12, plus 2.)

Row 1: Work 1 HDC in the 3rd chain from the hook. Work 1 HDC in each of the next 11 chains (12 HDC). On the 12th HDC, pull through with White. *Work 1 HDC in each of the next 12 chains carrying Vapor Gray along the row and crocheting over it. On the 12th HDC, pull through with Vapor Gray. Work 1 HDC in each of the next 12 chains carrying White along the row and crocheting over it. Repeat from * across the row. CH 2 and turn.

Row 2: *Work 1 WHDC in each of the next 12 spaces crocheting over White yarn. On the 12th stitch, pull through with White. Work 1 WHDC in each of the next 12 spaces carrying Vapor Gray along and crocheting over it. Repeat from * across the row. CH 2 and turn.

Repeat row 2 until you have 12 rows. On last stitch, pull through with Black. Cut White and Vapor Gray. Leave long tails to weave in later.

Row 13: *With Black, work 1 WHDC in each of the next 12 spaces, pull through with Misty Gray on the 12th stitch. Work 1 WHDC in each of the next 12 spaces, carry Black along, change color to Black on the 12th stitch. Repeat from * across the row, making sure to crochet over Misty Gray and carry along. CH 2 and turn.

Repeat row 13 until you have 12 rows of alternating Black and Misty Gray. Pull through with Vapor Gray on the last stitch. You may stop carrying the Mist Gray on the very last 12 stitches of the 12th row. Cut Misty Gray and Black. To hide yarn that might still be showing through, you can reach your hook underneath the carried yarn from the row below to tuck it up against the bottom of a row to hide it further.

Repeat rows 2 and 13 until you have 13 blocks of alternating colors. Weave in ends.

BORDER

Round 1: With Black, pull up a loop in any corner and work 1 HDC in each stitch around as evenly as possible. Work 3 HDC into each corner space. Join with a slip stitch to the first HDC, CH 2 and turn.

Round 2: Work 1 DC into each HDC stitch around, working 3 DC into each middle HDC of the corners. Join with a slip stitch to the turning chain, CH 2 and turn.

Round 3: Work alternating FPDC and BPDC around each DC. Work 3 alternating FPDC and BPDC around the middle DC of the corner. Join with a slip stitch to the turning chain, CH 2 and turn.

Rounds 4 - 5: Repeat round 3 making sure that you keep the post stitches facing the same direction as previous round. Join with a slip stitch at the end of round 5, then tie off and weave in ends.

-Tiffany

VELVET WINDOWPANE THROW

YARN

Bernat Velvet
100% polyester
300g/10.5 oz, 288 m/315 yds

COLORS

6 skeins Smokey Violet

TOOLS

Size J/6.00mm hook
Tapestry needle
Scissors

SIZE

42 in x 48 in

GAUGE

4 in = 12 st, 14 rows WHDC

STITCHES

Half Double Crochet (HDC)
Wide Half Double Crochet
(WHDC)
Double Crochet (DC)
Front and Back Post Double
Crochet (FPDC & BPDC)
Large Puff Stitch

PATTERN

-Keep your tension tight. Since this yarn is more slippery, having a tighter tension will help prevent stitches from coming loose. If you start this blanket and it seems like your stitches are not staying secure, you may want to try going down a hook size.

-When switching to a new skein, try to bring in the new yarn at the end of the row instead of the middle and knot the two ends together before you weave them into the blanket.

Chain 117. (Pattern repeat is a multiple of 20, plus 17.)

Row 1: Starting in the 3rd chain from the hook, work 1 HDC in each chain. CH 2 and turn.

Row 2: *Work 1 WHDC into each of the first 15 spaces, then work 1 Large Puff stitch, 1 WHDC, 1 Puff stitch, 1 WHDC, 1 Puff stitch. Repeat from * to the end of the row. CH 2 and turn.

Row 3: Work 1 WHDC into each space across the row. CH 2 and turn.

Rows 4 - 17: Repeat rows 2 and 3.

Row 18: *Work 1 WHDC into the first space, then work 1 Puff stitch into the next space. Repeat from * to the end of the row. CH 2 and turn.

Rows 19 - 22: Repeat rows 3 and 18.

Row 23: Repeat row 3.

Repeat rows 2 - 23 five more times. Weave in ends.

BORDER

Round 1: Pull up a loop in corner and CH 2. Work 1 round of DC around the blanket. Work DC, CH 1, DC into each corner space.

Round 2: At starting corner, work DC, CH 1 DC, then continue in same direction and work alternating FPDC and BPDC around each DC. Work DC, CH 1, DC in the chain 1 spaces of the corners. (Make sure and work the DC of the row below that makes the corner in the FP or BP that keeps the sequence alternating correctly.)

Rounds 3 - 4: Continue working in the same direction and repeat round 2. Always match your post DCs so that they are poking out in the same direction as the previous row. When you finish the last round of your border, slip stitch into the starting corner and tie off.

-Hannah

MESH AND RIBBED STITCH THROW

YARN

Bernat Forever Fleece Finer
100% polyester
280 g/9.9 oz, 352 m/385 yds

COLORS

6 skeins White Cloud

TOOLS

Size 7.00mm hook
Tapestry needle
Scissors

SIZE

40 in x 50 in

GAUGE

4 in = 12 st, 13 rows pattern

STITCHES

Single Crochet (SC)
Double Crochet (DC)
Front and Back Post Double
Crochet (FPDC & BPDC)
Half Double Slip Stitch
(HDSS)
Slip Stitch (SL ST)

VIDEO

PATTERN

Chain 120. (Pattern repeat is any multiple of 10.)

Row 1: Beginning in the 2nd chain from the hook, work 1 SC. SC into each of the next 8 chains. *DC into the next chain. SC into each of the next 9 chains. Repeat from * across the row. CH 1 and turn. (119)

Row 2: Starting in the 1st stitch, SC into SC of the previous row. CH 1, skip the next SC, SC into the next SC. (This is the Mesh Stitch sequence.) Mesh Stitch across the next 6 sts (your last SC will be just before the DC). *FPDC around the DC. Begin the Mesh Stitch in the next SC and across the next 8 sts. Repeat from * to the end of the row. CH 1 and turn.

Tip: The Mesh Stitch will be worked across 9 stitches beginning and ending with SC. You will omit the CH 1 on the 10th stitch and work the post DC. Always CH 1 and turn.

Row 3: *Work Mesh Stitch across first 9 stitches, BPDC around the next st. (Pop the post to the back of the work so the rib stays on the same side of the blanket.) Repeat from * across the row ending with the final 9 stitches being worked in the Mesh Stitch. CH 1 and turn.

Repeat rows 2 and 3 until blanket measures approximately 46 inches or to however long you'd like allowing for a 4 inch border.

BORDER

Round 1: Work 1 round of SC around the entire blanket working 3 SC into each corner. Don't turn or join at the end of the round.

First Side: CH 10. Work 1 HDSS in second chain from hook and into each of the next 8 chains, working back towards the edge of the blanket. SL ST into the next stitch on the blanket edge and the next st. Turn the border toward you, work HDSS into each HDSS. CH 1 and turn. (9 HDSS) Continue working the HDSS perpendicular across the first edge of blanket until it is even with the second side. End before you CH 1 and turn.

Tip: If the border is ruffling, try slip stitching 3 times, if the blanket is pulling, try slip stitching only once.

Second Side: Instead of CH 1 and turn, CH 10. Begin the border with HDSS into each of the next 9 chains. SL ST across the next 2 sts, turn and work HDSS into each HDSS. Work in the same manner as above.

Third and Fourth Side: Begin each side by chaining 10 and working in the same way as previous sides. After the fourth side, work 2 more rounds of SC with 3 SC into each corner. Join at the end of the round with a SL ST to the first SC, tie off and weave in all the ends.

-Tiffany

MODERN STRIPE THROW

. . . .

YARN

Patons Alpaca Blend
60% acrylic, 22% wool
10% nylon, 8% alpaca
100 g/3.5 oz, 142 m/155 yds

COLORS

9 skeins Lagoon
9 skeins Birch

TOOLS

Size J/6.00mm hook
Tapestry needle
Scissors

SIZE

42 in x 56 in

STITCHES

Half Double Crochet (HDC)
Half Double Slip Stitch
(HDSS)

PATTERN

Chain 200 with Lagoon (or any number).

Row 1: Starting in the 3rd chain from hook, work 1 HDC in each chain. CH 1 and turn.

Row 2: *Turning chain does not count as stitch.* Work 1 HDSS in the back loop only of each stitch to the end of the row. CH 1 and turn.

Repeat row 2 for the remainder of the blanket. CH 1 and turn.

Tip: You can choose to chain 2 after every row if you wish. I wanted the blanket to have a tighter, more knit look so I only chained one.

Color changes: 14 rows of Lagoon, 14 rows of Birch, 3 rows of Lagoon, 3 rows of Birch, 3 rows of Lagoon, 3 rows of Birch, 91 rows of Lagoon (about 6 1/2 skeins), 91 rows of Birch (about 6 1/2 skeins), 3 rows of Lagoon, 3 rows of Birch, 3 rows of Lagoon, 3 rows of Birch, 14 rows of Lagoon, 14 rows of Birch.

Weave in ends. Cut even pieces of yarn to create tassels and attach to corners.

-Nicolina

GIANT BASKETWEAVE THROW

YARN

Bernat Velvet Plus
100% polyester
300 g/10.5 oz, 71 m/78 yds

COLORS

9 skeins Cream

TOOLS

Size N/P/10.00mm hook
Tapestry needle
Scissors

SIZE

40 in x 52 in

STITCHES

Double Crochet (DC)
Front and Back Post Double
Crochet (FPDC & BPDC)

VIDEO

PATTERN

Chain 64.

Row 1: Starting in 4th chain from the hook, work 1 DC in each chain. CH 2 and turn.

Row 2: *Work FPDC around each of the next 12 DC.

(Tip: Your first FPDC to work is around the second post in the row below, not the post that lines up under the turning chain.)

Work BPDC around each of the next 12 DC. Repeat from * across the row. Work FPDC around the last 12 posts of the row, work 1 DC around the turning chain. CH 2 and turn.

Row 3: *Work BPDC around each of the next 12 posts. FPDC around each of the next 12. Repeat from * across the row. Work 1 DC around the turning chain.

Rows 4 - 11: Repeat rows 2 and 3.

Rows 12 - 21: Repeat rows 2 and 3, reversing the direction of the post stitches to create basketweave appearance. After finishing the next 10 rows, change the direction of the posts again. You will have 6 blocks high and 5 blocks wide total.

BORDER

When finished, work 1 round of DC around the blanket, working 1 DC into each stitch across the top and bottom, 3 DC into each corner and as evenly as possible around the stitches/turning chains on each side.

-Tiffany

RIBBED VELVET THROW

YARN

Bernat Velvet
100% polyester
300 g/10.5 oz, 288 m/315 yds

COLORS

5 skeins Smokey Green

TOOLS

Size I/5.50mm hook
Tapestry needle
Scissors

SIZE

36 in x 46 in

GAUGE

4 in = 12 st, 12 rows pattern

STITCHES

Double Crochet (DC)
Front and Back Post Double
Crochet (FPDC & BPDC)
Wide Half Double Crochet
(WHDC)

VIDEO

PATTERN

Chain 102. (Pattern repeat is an odd number multiplied by 2, plus 4.)

Row 1: Starting in the 4th chain from the hook, work 1 DC in each chain. CH 2 and turn.

Row 2: Work FPDC around the first two posts (not around the turning chain). Then work BPDC around the next two posts. Continue alternating 2 FPDC and 2 BPDC to the end of the row. At the end of the row work a regular DC, inserting your hook underneath the turning chain. CH 2 and turn.

Row 3: Work BPDC around the first two posts. Then FPDC around the next two posts. Continue alternating 2 BPDCs and 2 FPDCs to the end of the row. Then work a regular DC, inserting your hook underneath the turning chain. CH 2 and turn.

Rows 4 - 7: Repeat rows 2 and 3.

Rows 8 - 9: Repeat row 2.

Row 10: Repeat row 3.

Rows 11 - 16: Repeat rows 2 and 3.

Repeat rows 2 through 16 until blanket measure about 46 inches.

Essentially you are stacking the post DCs on top of each other for 8 rows and then changing directions for the next eight rows. I ended up with 14 sections of 8 rows when my blanket was the length I wanted.

BORDER

Round 1: Work one round of WHDC, inserting your hook in between the DC posts and the DC rows on the sides of the blanket. Work 3 HDCs in each corner.

Round 2: At starting corner, work 4 WHDCs in the corner, 2 on each side of the middle stitch from the 3 WHDCs you did on round 1. Continue working WHDC in between the posts around the blanket, putting 4 WHDCs in each corner in the same way you did the first corner.

Round 3: When you reach the corner you started with, work 3 WHDCs in the middle of the 4 stitches from round 2, so that there are 2 stitches on each side of the 3 new stitches. Continue working WHDC in between the posts around the blanket, working 3 WHDCs in each corner.

Rounds 4 - 7: Continue alternating rounds 2 and 3 until you reach your desired border height. When you finish the border, slip stitch into the starting corner and tie off.

-Hannah

MODERN MOSS STITCH THROW

YARN

Caron One Pound
100% acrylic
454 g/16 oz, 742 m/812 yds

COLORS

2 skeins White
1 skein Black

TOOLS

Size J/6.00mm hook
Tapestry needle
Scissors

SIZE

40 in x 53 in

GAUGE

4 in = 8 st, 14 rows pattern

STITCHES

Single Crochet (SC)

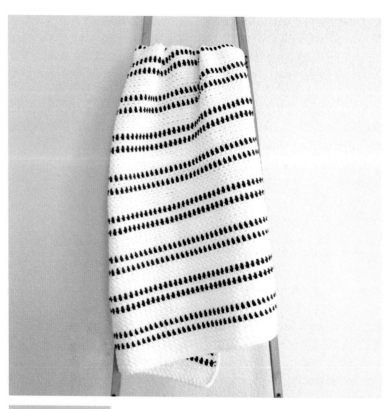

PATTERN

Chain 150 with White. (Pattern repeat is any even number.)

Row 1: Starting in the 4th chain from the hook, work SC, CH 1. *Skip one chain, then SC, CH 1 in the next chain. Repeat from * until the last chain. Work 1 SC into the last chain, then CH 2 and turn.

Rows 2 - 8: Insert your hook into the first chain one space from the previous row, and SC, CH 1. Work SC, CH 1 into each chain one space across the row (moss stitch). Work the last SC into the space between the last SC and turning chain of the row below. CH 2 and turn. At the end of row 8, pull through with Black before you finish the last SC, then CH 2 and turn.

Tip: At this point you can either cut the White yarn and leave a long tail to weave into the blanket later, or you can bring it with you as you work the next row in Black, by laying the White across the top of your work and crocheting over it as you go. I chose to always carry the White yarn and crochet over it each time I worked a black row so I could easily pick it up on the other side, and I always cut the Black and left tails to weave in at the end.

Row 9: With Black, work SC, CH 1 into each chain one space across the row. At the end of the row, pull through with White before you finish the last SC. CH 2 with White and turn (cut the Black).

Rows 10 - 12: With White, work SC, CH 1 into each chain one space across the row. Work 1 SC into final space, CH 2 and turn. At the end of row 12, pull through with Black, CH 2 and turn.

Row 13: Repeat row 9.

Rows 14 - 21: With White, work SC, CH 1 into each chain one space across the row. Work 1 SC into final space, CH 2 and turn.

Repeat rows 9 through 21 until your blanket measures 50 to 55 inches. In simple terms, the color pattern I used is 8 rows White, 1 row Black, 3 rows White, 1 row Black.

BORDER

Round 1: With White, pull up a loop in any corner and CH 2. Work the moss stitch (SC, CH 1, skip 1) around the sides and ends of the blanket. Work 3 SC into each corner. When you reach the corner you started with, slip stitch into the starting stitch, then CH 2 and turn.

Round 2: Continue working the moss stitch around the blanket in the opposite direction. When you reach the starting corner, slip stitch into the corner and tie off.

-Hannah

INVERSE SQUARES THROW

YARN

Red Heart with Love
100% acrylic
198 g/7 oz, 338 m/370 yds

COLORS

4 skeins Black
4 skeins Aran

TOOLS

Size J/6.00mm hook
Tapestry needle
Scissors

SIZE

44 in x 60 in

GAUGE

4 in = 12 st, 10 rows pattern

STITCHES

Single Crochet (SC)
Double Crochet (DC)

VIDEO

PATTERN

Chain 141 with Aran. (Pattern repeat is a multiple of 20, plus 1.)

Row 1: Reading the graph right to left starting in the bottom right-hand corner marked (1), begin in the second chain from the hook with 1 SC. Work 1 DC into the next chain. *Work 1 SC into the next chain and 1 DC into the next. Repeat from * across the chain making color changes according to the graph. After finishing 40 stitches across, start at stitch 1 and repeat the graph 2 and a half more times. End with 1 repeat of stitches 1 through 20. You will have 7 blocks across. CH 1 and turn.

Tip: Carry the color not being used along the row with you and crochet over it. Always change color in the last step of the stitch and pull through with new color. Give this a little tug before doing so to make sure the carried yarn is laying flat against the row. It is normal to see the color through the work, but make it lay flat and not poke through the stitches.

Row 2: Reading the graph from left to right starting with the row marked 2, begin in the first stitch with *1 SC into the top of the first DC in the row previous. Work 1 DC into the next SC stitch of the row previous. Repeat from * across the row following the color changes in the graph. CH 1 and turn.

Tip: The even rows always are the same color changes as the previous row.

Rows 3 - 36: Following the graph and using the griddle stitch throughout, make the color changes as noted. After completing row 36 of the graph, begin with row 1 and repeat. The blanket is finished when there are 8 blocks high.

BORDER

Round 1: After making the last block of the graph, with Aran, CH 1 and turn. Work 1 SC into each stitch across the top of the blanket. Work 3 SC into the last stitch and turn to work down the side. Work 1 SC at the end of each row that ends with a SC and work 2 SC into the end of the rows that end with a DC. Work 3 SC into the last stitch of the row and turn to work the bottom/starting row of the blanket. Work 1 SC into each stitch across the bottom. Work 3 SC into the last stitch and turn to work up the final side of the blanket in the same manner as the first side you worked. Join with a slip stitch to the first SC after working 2 SC into the corner, CH 1 and continue in the same direction.

Round 2: Work 1 SC into each SC around, working 3 SC into each corner SC. Join with a slip stitch into the first SC of the round. Tie off and weave in all the ends.

-Tiffany

WINTER WEAR

EASY CROCHET BEANIE

YARN

Caron Simply Soft
100% acrylic
170 g/6 oz, 288 m/315 yds

COLORS

1 skein any color

TOOLS

Size H/5.00mm hook
Tapestry needle
Scissors

OPTIONAL

Hat Label

STITCHES

Slip Stitch (SL ST)
Single Crochet (SC)

VIDEO

PATTERN

Make a chain to the length of the hat height that you need. For my baby grandson Jack I made the chain 10 inches long and chained 40.

When calculating base chain, adding three inches to the measurement of the tip of the nose to the crown of the head is a good guideline. This will make sure you have enough for the brim to fold up. If you want a slouchy hat, add even more length to the base chain.

Row 1: Beginning in the 2nd chain from the hook, work 1 SL ST under the back loop. Work 1 SL ST into each of the next 4 chains. SC into each chain to the end. CH 1 and turn.

Row 2: Work 1 SC into the back loop of each SC. Work 1 SL ST into the back loop of each of the remaining 5 stitches. CH 1 and turn. (Keep your slip stitches loose, especially the last one before you chain and turn.)

Row 3: Work 1 SL ST into the back loop of each SL ST. Work 1 SC into the back loop of each SC to the end of the row. CH 1 and turn.

Repeat rows 2 and 3 until the hat measures 3 inches less that the circumference of the head. For my grandson Jack this was about 62 rows. He has a 17 inch head circumference.

End the last row on row 2 instructions so the tail is at the top of the hat.

Tie off leaving a long tail for sewing. Weave in and out of the top of the hat to gather close, then sew the two sides together.

Tie off and weave in the ends. Roll up the brim and attach label.

-Tiffany

Easy Crochet Beanie	if your head circumference measures this:	then make the hat height (base chain) this:	and make the width of your hat this:
Preemie	12-13 in	8 in	9-10 in
Newborn-3 Months	13-14 in	8 in	10-11 in
3-6 Months	14-15 in	9 in	11-12 in
6-12 Months	15-16 in	9.5 in	12-13 in
12-24 Months	16-18 in	10 in	13-15 in
Child (3-10 years)	19-21 in	11 in	16-17 in
Teen/Small Adult	21 in	11 in	18 in
Medium Adult	22 in	11.5 in	19 in
Large Adult	23 in	12 in	20 in

BEGINNER COLORFUL SCARVES

YARN

Patons Alpaca Blend
60% acrylic, 22% wool
10% nylon, 8% alpaca
100g/3.5oz, 142 m/155 yds

COLORS

For one scarf
2 skeins Yam, Butternut
or Petunia

TOOLS

Size J/6.00mm hook
Tapestry needle
Scissors

SIZE

70 in x 5 in (including tassels)

STITCHES

Half Double Crochet (HDC)
Half Double Slip Stitch
(HDSS)

VIDEO

PATTERN

Chain 185, or a chain that measures the desired length of your scarf.

Row 1: Starting in the 3rd chain from the hook, work 1 HDC into each chain. CH 2 and turn.

Row 2: *The turning chain does not count as a stitch.* Work 1 HDSS into each stitch across the row. CH 2 and turn.

Row 3: Work 1 HDC into each stitch across the row. CH 2 and turn.

Repeat rows 2 through 3 until your scarf measures about 5 inches wide.

For a variation of this pattern, try working in the front loop only or the back loop only.

When you finish your scarf, tie off and weave in all ends with a tapestry needle. If you'd like you can add tassels by cutting about 40 ten inch pieces of yarn and tying them to each end of your scarf.

To make a tassel, take two pieces of yarn and fold them in half, then insert the folded end through a space on the end of your scarf. Pull out the folded end so that it makes a loop, then pull the ends through the loop and pull tightly to make a knot.

-Hannah

EASY VELVET TWIST HEADBAND

YARN

Bernat Baby Velvet
100% polyester
3.5 oz/100 g, 149 m/163 yds

COLORS

1 skein any color

TOOLS

Size H/5.00mm hook
Tapestry needle
Scissors

SIZE

Can be made in any size

STITCHES

Wide Half Double Crochet
(WHDC)

VIDEO

AVERAGE HEAD CIRCUMFERENCE	
Preemie	12-13 in
Newborn-3M	13-14 in
3-6M	14-15 in
6-12M	15-16 in
12-24M	16-18 in
Child (3 - 10)	19-21 in
Teen/Small Adult	21 in
Medium Adult	22 in
Large Adult	23 in

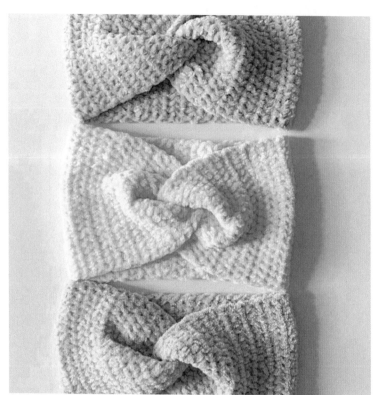

86

PATTERN

Chain 20. (Chain 16 for children under the age of 5.)

Row 1: Starting in the 3rd chain from the hook, work 1 HDC into each chain. CH 2 and turn. (18 st)

Row 2: Work 1 WHDC into each space across the row. Your last WHDC will be worked in between the post and the turning chain. CH 2 and turn.

Repeat row 2 until your headband measures 19.5 inches for an average woman's size head or to the size you need. (Make your headband about 3 inches smaller than head circumference.)

TWIST

Step 1: Lay the band out and fold in half and slide one side of the band across so one end is matched up to the middle of the other.

Step 2: Fold the right hand side around the back.

Step 3: Fold the left hand side around the front, giving you four layers

Step 4: Sew with the tapestry needle through all four layers.

-Tiffany

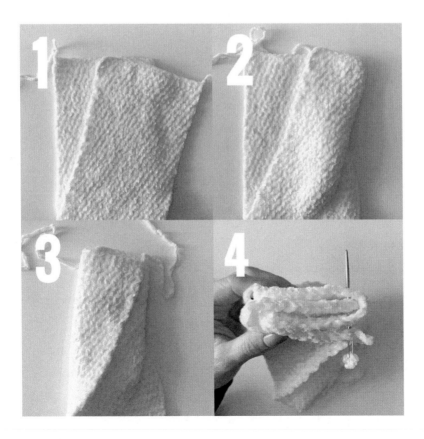

BABY T HAT

YARN

Caron Simply Soft
100% acrylic
170 g/6 oz, 288 m/315 yds

COLORS

1 skein White
1 skein Persimmon
1 skein Light Country Peach
1 skein Light Country Blue
1 skein Country Blue

TOOLS

Size H/5.00mm hook
Size G/4.00mm hook
Tapestry needle
Scissors
Tape Measure
Pom pom maker

SIZE

Can be made in any size

STITCHES

Single Crochet (SC)

VIDEO

PATTERN

Gauge for the brim: 18 SC and 20 rows = 4 in with G hook
Gauge for the hat: 20 SC and 22 rows = 4 in with H hook

Brim: With White and size G hook, **chain 7** for baby sizes, **chain 9** for older child to adult.

Row 1: Starting in the 2nd chain from the hook, work 1 SC in each chain. CH 1 and turn.

Row 2: Work 1 SC into the first stitch. 1 SC into the back loop of each of the next 4 stitches. 1 SC into the last stitch. CH 1 and turn.

Repeat row 2 until your band measures 12 inches for a newborn size. Or refer to the chart below for the size you need. Don't tie off but mark the stitch as a place holder. Remove your hook while you join the band with your tapestry needle and sew the ends together forming a circle.

Round 1: *Change to your size H hook.* Return to the marked stitch and turn the band so that you are working into the side of of the first row of SC made for the brim. Work 1 SC into that space. Work 2 SC into the end of the next row. *Skip one row, work 2 SC into the end of the next row. Repeat from * around the edge of the circle. Join with a slip stitch to the first SC. CH 1 and turn.

Round 2: Work 1 SC into the first SC. *CH 1, skip the next stitch, 1 SC into the next stitch. Repeat from * around. Join with a slip stitch, CH 1 and turn.

Repeat round 2 until your hat measures 5 inches for the newborn size, 9 inches for an adult size, or refer to the chart for other sizes.

For the adult size hat I worked 2 rows White, 8 rows Persimmon, 3 rows Light Country Peach, 4 rows Country Blue, 2 rows Light Country Blue, 7 rows White, 4 Rows Persimmon, 8 rows Light Country Peach, 2 rows Country Blue, 4 rows Light Country Blue. When your hat reaches the desired height, tie off and leave a long tail to gather the top of the hat. Use your tapestry needle to weave the tail in and out of stitches along the top of the hat, then pull tightly to gather the hat in. Then tie off and weave in ends. Attach a pom pom if you choose and you're done! *-Tiffany*

Baby T Hat	if your head circumference measures this:	then make the brim of your hat this:	and make the hat height this:
Preemie	12-13 in	10-11 in	4 in
Newborn-3 Months	13-14 in	11-12 in	5-5.5 in
3-6 Months	14-15 in	12-13 in	6 in
6-12 Months	15-16 in	13-14 in	6.5 in
12-24 Months	16-18 in	14-16 in	6.5-7 in
Child (3-10 years)	19-21 in	17-19 in	7.5-8 in
Teen/Small Adult	21 in	19 in	8 in
Medium Adult	22 in	20 in	8.5 in
Large Adult	23 in	21 in	8.5-9 in

CHUNKY COLOR DIPPED SCARF

YARN

Bernat Softee Chunky
100% acrylic
100 g/3.5 oz, 99 m/108 yds

COLORS

2 skeins Gray Ragg
1 skein Sea Green

TOOLS

Size L/8.00mm hook
Tapestry needle
Scissors

SIZE

6 in x 80 in

STITCHES

Single Crochet (SC)

PATTERN

Chain 18 with Sea Green. (Pattern repeat is any even number.)

Row 1: SC in the 2nd chain from the hook and CH 1. Skip one chain, then SC, CH 1. Skip the next chain and continue the pattern of SC, CH 1, SK 1 all the way across. When you reach the end of the row and make the last SC, CH 1 and turn.

Row 2: SC into the SC you just made on the row below. CH 1, skip the chain space, SC into the SC. Repeat the sequence all the way across. Ending again with a SC in the last SC. CH 1 and turn.

Rows 3 - 24: Repeat row 2 with Sea Green. On the 24th row, on the last stitch, pull through on the last step of the SC with Gray Ragg.

Rows 25 - 112: Repeat row 2. On the 112th row, on the last stitch, pull through on the last step of the SC with Sea Green.

Rows 113 - 136: Repeat row 2. Tie off and weave in all the ends.

-Haley

CABLE TWIST HAT

YARN

Patons Wool Roving
100% wool
100 g/3.5 oz, 109 m/120 yds

COLORS

2 skeins any color

TOOLS

Size J/6.00mm hook
Tapestry needle
Scissors

OPTIONAL

Faux fur pom pom

SIZE

Average women's size head

STITCHES

Half Double Crochet (HDC)
Wide Half Double Crochet
(WHDC)
Double Crochet (DC)
Front and Back Post Double
Crochet (FPDC & BPDC)
Front Post Treble Crochet
(FPTC)
Single Crochet 2 Together
(SC2TOG)

VIDEO

PATTERN

Chain 59. (Pattern repeat is a multiple of 8, plus 3.)

Row 1: Starting in the 3rd chain from hook, *work 1 HDC. 1 DC in each of the next 2 chains. HDC in next chain. 1 DC in each of the next 4 chains. Repeat from * across until 1 chain remains, HDC in last chain. CH 2 and turn.

Row 2: *WHDC in the first space. FPDC around each of the next 4 DC. WHDC in next space, FPDC around the next 2 DC. Repeat from * to the last 2 DC, end with 1 WHDC. CH 2 and turn.

Row 3: *WHDC, BPDC around next 2 posts. WHDC, BPDC around next 4 posts. Repeat * and end with 1 WHDC (it's always worked in between the last stitch and the turning chain). CH 2 and turn.

Row 4: (Cable twist row) *WHDC, Skip the next three DC and FPTC around the 4th DC. FPTC around the third DC, FPDC around the second DC, FPDC around the first DC. Twist and reach over to work the next WHDC, FPDC around next 2 posts. Repeat from * and end with one WHDC in between the last stitch and the turning chain. CH 2 and turn.

Row 5: Repeat row 3.

Row 6: Repeat row 2.

Row 7: Repeat row 3.

Row 8: Repeat row 4.

Rows 9 - 16: Repeat rows 5 - 8.

Rows 17 - 18: Repeat rows 3 and 2. At the end of row 18, CH 1 and turn.

Rows 19 - 21: SC2TOG across every two stitches to decrease and gather the top of the hat. CH 1 and turn after each row. Cut off leave a long tail and continue gathering in the top of the hat with a tapestry needle and sew the two sides together. Weave in all ends.

Attach a pom pom. Methods to try are sewing a button on the underside of the hat and threading the tails (or elastic on pom) and tying around the button. Or find a pom with snaps attached.

-Tiffany

RIBBED VELVET TWIST HEADBAND

YARN

Bernat Baby Velvet
100% polyester
3.5 oz/100 g, 149 m/163 yds

COLORS

1 skein any color

HOOK

Size H/5.00mm hook

TOOLS

Tapestry needle
Scissors

SIZE

Can be made in any size

STITCHES

Double Crochet (DC)
Front and Back Post Double
Crochet (FPDC & BPDC)

AVERAGE HEAD CIRCUMFERENCE

Preemie	12-13 in
Newborn-3M	13-14 in
3-6M	14-15 in
6-12M	15-16 in
12-24M	16-18 in
Child (3 - 10)	19-21 in
Teen/Small Adult	21 in
Medium Adult	22 in
Large Adult	23 in

PATTERN

Chain 20 for adults, 18 for kids, or 16 for babies.

Row 1: Starting in the 4th chain from the hook, work 1 DC in each chain. CH 2 and turn.

Row 2: The chain 2 counts as the first stitch. Around the next stitch, work a FPDC. Around the next stitch, work a BPDC. Continue alternating FPDC and BPDC to the end of the row. When you reach the end of the row, work a regular DC underneath the turning chain. CH 2 and turn.

Row 3: The chain 2 counts as the first stitch. Continue alternating BPDC and FPDC to the end of the row, always matching the direction you work around the post so that it pops out the same direction as the previous row. When you reach the end of the row, work a regular DC underneath the turning chain. CH 2 and turn.

Repeat rows 2 through 3 until headband measures 3 inches less than head circumference. If you are not able to measure in person, use head chart for average head sizes.

TWIST

Step 1: Lay the band out and fold in half and slide one side of the band across so one end is matched up to the middle of the other.

Step 2: Fold the right hand side around the back.

Step 3: Fold the left hand side around the front, giving you four layers

Step 4: Sew with the tapestry needle through all four layers.

-Hannah

CLUSTER STITCH INFINITY SCARF

YARN

Patons Alpaca Blend
60% acrylic, 22% wool
10% nylon, 8% alpaca
100g/3.5oz, 142 m/155 yds

COLORS

2 skeins Butternut

TOOLS

Size J/6.00mm hook
Tapestry needle
Scissors

SIZE

Average adult-sized scarf

STITCHES

Single Crochet (SC)
Half Double Crochet (HDC)
HDC Cluster (HDC-CL)

PATTERN

Chain 170. (Pattern repeat is any even number.)

Row 1: Starting in the 3rd chain from the hook, work 1 HDC in each chain. CH 2 and turn.

Row 2: Work 1 HDC in the front two loops of each stitch across the row. CH 2 and turn.

Row 3: In the first stitch of the row below, working in the front two loops, *HDC-CL. SC in the front two loops of the next stitch. Repeat from * across the row. CH 2 and turn.

Row 4: Work 1 HDC in the front loop of each stitch across the row. CH 2 and turn.

Rows 5 - 6: Repeat row 2.

Row 7: Repeat row 3.

Row 8: Repeat row 4.

Rows 9 - 10: Repeat row 2.

Row 11: Repeat row 3

Row 12: Repeat row 4.

Rows 13 - 14: Repeat row 2.

When you finish the last row, you can either tie off and leave a long tail to sew the two sides of the scarf together with a tapestry needle, or you can slip stitch the two sides together.

If you decide to slip stitch them together, then you'll want to make sure that the backside of the scarf is facing outward so that you can turn it inside out after you're finished and the thicker seam will be on the inside.

Weave in ends when finished.

-Hannah

VINTAGE STRIPES BEANIE

YARN

Caron Simply Soft
100% acrylic
170 g/6 oz, 288 m/315 yds

COLORS

1 skein each Off White,
Charcoal Heather, Sage,
Gold, Harvest Red

TOOLS

Size H/5.00mm hook
Tapestry needle
Scissors

OPTIONAL

Pom pom maker or
Faux fur pom pom

GAUGE

2 in = 8 st, 6 rows HHDC

STITCHES

Herringbone Half Double
Crochet (HHDC)
Double Crochet (DC)
Front and Back Post Double
Crochet (FPDC & BPDC)

VIDEO

PATTERN

Work this pattern according to the size chart if you are using different yarn or making adult size. Stitch counts in pattern following is for a size child age 3 - 10.

With Off White, make a magic circle.

Round 1: CH 2, work 8 HHDC in circle, join with a slip stitch to first stitch. Do not turn. (8)

Round 2: CH 2, work 2 HHDC in each HHDC, pull Charcoal Heather through with slip stitch. (16)

Round 3: CH 2. *Work 2 HHDC in the first stitch, 1 HHDC in next stitch. Repeat from *. Join with a slip stitch to the first stitch. (24)

Round 4: CH 2. *Work 2 HHDC, 1 HHDC in each of the next 2 stitches. Repeat from *. Join with a slip stitch to the first stitch pulling through with Off White. (32)

Round 5: CH 2. *2 HHDC, 1 HHDC in each of the next 3 stitches. Repeat from *. Join with a slip stitch to the first stitch. (40)

Round 6: CH 2. *2 HHDC, 1 HHDC in each of the next 4 stitches. Repeat from *. Join with a slip stitch to first stitch pulling through with Gold. (48)

Round 7: CH 2. *2 HHDC, 1 HHDC in each of the next 5 stitches. Repeat from *. Join with a slip stitch to the first stitch. (56)

Round 8: CH 2. *2 HHDC, 1 HHDC in each of the next 6 stitches. Repeat from *. Join with a slip stitch to the first stitch pulling through with Off White. (64)

Round 9: CH 2. * 2 HHDC, 1 HHDC in each of the next 7 stitches. Repeat from *. Join with a slip stitch to the first stitch. (72) *Measure the width of the circle and refer to the size chart; if you need to add one or two more rows, continue with the same sequence of increases.*

Round 10: CH 2. Work 1 HHDC in each stitch around. Join with a slip stitch pulling through with Harvest Red. (72)

Rounds 11 - 24: Repeat the instructions for round 10, changing colors every 2 rows using Off White, Sage, Off White, Charcoal Heather, Off White, Gold.

Rounds 25 - 27: Brim of hat. With Off White, CH 2 and work 1 (DC) in each stitch around, join with a slip stitch to the chain 2. Do not turn, *work 1 FPDC around the next DC and then work 1 BPDC around the next DC. Repeat from * around. Join with a slip stitch to the chain 2 at the end of each round. On the third round, work FPDC around each FPDC and BPDC around BPDC to form a ribbed look.

Tie off and weave in all ends at the end of round 27. Attach a pom pom and you're done!

-Tiffany

Vintage Stripes Beanie	if your head circumference measures this:	then make the crown circle diameter this:	and make the hat height this:
Preemie	12-13 in	3-3.5 in	4-4.5 in
Newborn-3 Months	13-14 in	4-4.5 in	5-5.5 in
3-6 Months	14-15 in	5 in	6 in
6-12 Months	15-16 in	5-5.5 in	6.5 in
12-24 Months	16-18 in	5.5-6 in	7 in
Child (3-10 years)	19-21 in	6-6.5 in	7.5-8 in
Teen/Small Adult	21 in	6.5-7 in	8-8.5 in
Medium Adult	22 in	7-7.5 in	8.5-9 in
Large Adult	23 in	8 in	9-9.5 in

VELVET MITTENS

YARN

Bernat Baby Velvet
100% polyester
3.5 oz/100 g, 149 m/163 yds

COLORS

2 skeins any color

TOOLS

Size H/5.00mm hook
Tapestry needle
Scissors

SIZE

Medium women's size

GAUGE

2 in = 7 st, 7 rows HDSS

STITCHES

Half Double Crochet (HDC)
Half Double Slip Stitch
(HDSS)

VIDEO

PATTERN

Chain 20, leaving a long tail (at least 36 inches) to use to sew the two sides together.

Row 1: Work HDSS in 2nd chain from hook and into each chain to the end. CH 1 and turn. (19)

Rows 2 - 28: Work HDSS in each st. CH 1 and turn. (19) Mark your stitch, sew the two ends together forming a circle.

Return to stitch, work 30 HDC around the top. Slip stitch to beginning HDC. CH 1 and turn.

Rounds 2 - 8: HDSS into each stitch going around, slip stitch to beginning stitch, CH 1 and turn. (30)

Tip: before you join with a slip stitch and turn, count your stitches. You should have made 30 HDSS. This will help you keep the mitten even as you work.

Round 9: Work 1 HDSS into each of the next 8 stitches. 2 HDSS in each of the next 2 stitches. Skip over the next 9 stitches. Work 2 HDSS in each of the next 2 stitches. Work 1 HDSS in each of the next 8 stitches. Join with a slip stitch, CH 1 and turn. (24)

Rounds 10 - 25: Work 1 HDSS into each of the next 24 stitches. CH 1 and turn.

Tie off with a long tail. Use a tapestry needle to gather the end of the thumb closed.

Weave in and secure the tail.

THUMB

Round 1: Pull up a loop on the mitten side of the hole. CH 1 and HDSS in the same space. Work 1 HDSS into each of the next 11 stitches. Join with a slip stitch to the first HDSS. (12 st)

Rounds 2 - 9: Work 1 HDSS into each stitch around, slip stitch to the first stitch, CH 1 and turn. Tie off with a long tail. Use a tapestry needle to gather the end of the thumb closed. Weave in and secure the tail.

-Tiffany

SPIRAL FRONT LOOP SC HAT

YARN

Bernat Roving
80% acrylic, 20% wool
100 g/3.5 oz, 109 m/120 yds

COLORS

1 skein any color (1 optional extra skein for pom pom)

TOOLS

Size M/N/9.00mm hook
Tapestry needle
Scissors
Stitch marker

OPTIONAL

Pom pom maker or
Faux fur pom pom

SIZE

Medium women's size

GAUGE

4 in = 9 st, 9 rows SC

STITCHES

Single Crochet (SC)

VIDEO

PATTERN

Start with a magic circle and work 8 SC into the loop. Pull together and place stitch marker around the 8th stitch. Work into the front loop of each SC now and throughout the rest of the pattern.

Round 1: Work 2 SC into each front loop of the SC from the row below. (16 SC) Place marker into the 16th stitch.

Round 2: Work *2 SC in next stitch, 1 SC in next, repeat from * around to the marker. (24 SC) Place marker into the 24th stitch.

Round 3: Work *2 SC in next stitch, 1 SC into each of the next 2 stitches. Repeat from * around to the marker. (32 SC) Place marker into the 32nd stitch.

Round 4: Work *2 SC in next stitch, 1 SC in each of the next 3 stitches. Repeat from * around to the marker. (40 SC) Place marker into the 40th stitch.

Rounds 5 - 14: Work 1 SC into each stitch. Leave stitch marker in so on the 14th row you will know when the round is complete. Slip stitch to next stitch, tie off and weave in the ends. Attach a pom pom.

Note: Working 14 rows is adjustable. Start trying on the hat around row 12, or add more rows if you'd like a brim that turns up.

-Tiffany

LINKED STITCH HAT

YARN

Sugar Bush Crisp
100% superwash marino
50 g/1.75 oz, 87 m/95 yds

COLORS

for 1 baby-sized hat
2 skeins French Blue

TOOLS

Size H/5.00mm hook
Tapestry needle
Scissors

OPTIONAL

Pom pom maker or
Faux fur pom pom

SIZE

Baby size, or see size chart

STITCHES

Single Crochet (SC)
Slip Stitch (SL ST)
Linked Stitch

PATTERN

Linked Stitch: CH 5. Insert your hook into the 2nd chain from the hook, YO and pull a loop back through, *insert your hook into the next chain, YO and pull a loop back through. Repeat from * two more times, until all chains are worked. YO and pull through two loops 4 times and until you have one loop remaining on the hook. To begin the next stitch, instead of working into chains, look for the horizontal bar and front loop of the corresponding stitch.

Brim - Chain 5.

Row 1: In the 2nd chain from the hook, work 1 SC. SC into each chain across the row. CH 1 and turn. (4)

Row 2: SC into the first stitch of the row. Work back loop SC into each of the next 2 stitches. SC into the last stitch. CH 1 and turn.

Rows 3 to 2 inches shorter than head circumference needed: Repeat row 2 (refer to the size chart).

When your band is the length you need, CH 1 and turn band so you are working along one long end.

Work 1 SC into the end of the first row. Skip one row, work 2 SC into the next row, repeat from * to the end. (Work into the dips or valleys at the end of a row and skip over the peak rows.)

Hat - chain 5.

Work linked stitch. Insert your hook into the 2nd chain from the hook, YO, pull a loop through, insert your hook and pull up a loop into each of the next three chains. Insert your hook into the SC on the band. YO and pull through two loops 5 times.

*Work linked stitch underneath the horizontal bar and front loop of corresponding stitch 4 times. Insert hook final time underneath the next SC on the band. YO and pull through two loops 5 times. Repeat from * across the row. CH 5 and turn.

Work linked stitch across the row.

Work 5 rows of linked stitch.

You may choose to slip stitch your two sides together or use your tapestry needle to sew the two ends together.

Gather the top of your hat by weaving your tapestry needle in and out of the front loop of each stitch, pull tight to close.

Attach a pom pom.

-Tiffany

Linked Stitch Hat	if your head circumference measures this:	then make the brim of your hat this:	and make the hat height this:
Preemie	12-13 in	10-11 in	4 in
Newborn-3 Months	13-14 in	11-12 in	5-5.5 in
3-6 Months	14-15 in	12-13 in	6 in
6-12 Months	15-16 in	13-14 in	6.5 in
12-24 Months	16-18 in	14-16 in	6.5-7 in
Child (3-10 years)	19-21 in	17-19 in	7.5-8 in
Teen/Small Adult	21 in	19 in	8 in
Medium Adult	22 in	20 in	8.5 in
Large Adult	23 in	21 in	8.5-9 in

DREAMY TEXTURED SCARF

YARN

Red Heart Dreamy
100% acrylic
250 g/8.8 oz, 426 m/466 yds

COLORS

2 skeins Buff

TOOLS

Size K/6.50mm hook
Scissors
Tapestry needle

SIZE

9.5 in x 78 in

GAUGE

2 in = 6 st, 5 rows pattern

STITCHES

Herringbone Half Double
Crochet (HHDC)
Half Double Crochet Cluster
(HDC-CL)

VIDEO

PATTERN

Chain 30. (Pattern repeat is any even number.)

Row 1: Starting in the 3rd chain from the hook, work 1 HHDC in each chain. CH 1 and turn. (29 st)

Row 2: In the first stitch, *work 1 HDC-CL. In the next stitch work 1 SC. Repeat from * across the row. CH 1 and turn.

Row 3: As row 2.

Rows 4 - 6: In the first stitch, work 1 HHDC. Work 1 HHDC in each stitch across. CH 1 and turn.

Repeat rows 2 through 6 until scarf measures approximately 75 inches. Then repeat rows 2 and 3 and finish with one row of HHDC.

Weave in all ends, cut 25 inch sections of yarn for the fringe and attach one piece per stitch on both ends of the scarf.

To attach fringe, fold each piece of yarn in half, feed the folded end through the stitch about 1/4 of the way, then reach through the loop, grab the tails and pull them through the loop to tighten.

-Tiffany

MESH AND BERRY HAT

YARN

Caron Simply Soft
100% acrylic
170 g/6 oz 288 m/315 yds

COLORS

1 skein each Off White,
Victorian Rose, Gold,
Sage, Gray Heather

TOOLS

Size 4.50mm hook
Size H/5.00mm hook
Scissors
Tapestry needle
Measuring tape

OPTIONAL

Pom pom maker or
Faux fur pom pom

SIZE

Any size - see size chart

STITCHES

Single Crochet (SC)
Berry Stitch

VIDEO

PATTERN

Brim: With Off White and size 4.5mm hook, CH 10. (Leave a long tail to use to sew the brim together.)

Row 1: Work 1 SC in the 2nd chain from the hook. 1 SC in each chain across the row. CH 1 and turn. (9)

Row 2: Work 1 SC under both loops in the first stitch, 1 SC in the back loop of each of the next 7 stitches. 1 SC in both loops of the last stitch. CH 1 and turn.

Row 3: Repeat row 2 until your band measures the size you need. Refer to the size chart.

Don't tie off but mark the stitch as a place holder. Remove your hook while you join the band with your tapestry needle and sew the ends together forming a circle.

Hat Round 1: *Change to your size H hook.* Return to the marked stitch and turn the band so that you are working into the side of the first row of SC made for the brim. Work 1 SC into that space. Work 2 SC into the end of the next row. *Skip one row, work 2 SC into the end of the next row. Repeat from * around the edge of the circle. Join with a slip stitch to the first SC. CH 1 and turn.

Round 2: Work 1 SC into the first SC. *CH 1, skip the next stitch, 1 SC into the next stitch. Repeat from * around. Join with a slip stitch, CH 1 and turn.

Round 3: Repeat instructions for round 2, pulling through with new color on the slip stitch, CH 1 and turn.

Round 4: (Berry Stitch Round) Work 1 SC into the first SC. *Berry Stitch into the ch 1 space. 1 SC into the next stitch. Repeat from * around. Join with a slip stitch pulling the Off White through to change colors.

Rounds 5 - 9: Repeat round 2 instructions for 5 rows, on last round pull through with new color.

Repeat round 4 and rounds 5 - 9 three more times.

First Decrease Round: Work 1 SC into each SC around. Join with a slip stitch to first stitch, CH 1 and turn.

Second Decrease Round: Work 1 SC into first SC, *skip one SC, work 1 SC into the next SC. Repeat from * around. Join with a slip stitch, CH 1 and turn.

Tie off and leave a long tail for sewing. Gather the hat the rest of the way in by using your tapestry needle and weaving in and out of last row of SC. Pull tight and weave in the end. Attach a pom pom.

-Tiffany

Mesh and Berry Hat	if your head circumference measures this:	then make the brim of your hat this:	and make the hat height this:
Preemie	12-13 in	10-11 in	4 in
Newborn-3 Months	13-14 in	11-12 in	5-5.5 in
3-6 Months	14-15 in	12-13 in	6 in
6-12 Months	15-16 in	13-15 in	6.5 in
12-24 Months	16-18 in	14-16 in	6.5-7 in
Child (3-10 years)	19-21 in	17-19 in	7.5-8 in
Teen/Small Adult	21 in	19 in	8 in
Medium Adult	22 in	20 in	8.5 in
Large Adult	23 in	21 in	8.5-9 in

HOUNDSTOOTH HAT

YARN

Red Heart Soft
100% acrylic
141 g/5 oz, 234 m/256 yds

COLORS

1 skein Black
1 skein White

TOOLS

Size I/5.50mm hook
Scissors
Tapestry needle

OPTIONAL

Pom pom maker or
Faux fur pom pom

SIZE

Medium women's size

STITCHES

Single Crochet (SC)
Double Crochet (DC)
Double Crochet 2 Together
(DC2TOG)
Slip Stitch (SL ST)

VIDEO

PATTERN

Band: With White, chain 15, leaving a long tail to use to sew the two ends together when finished with band.

Row 1: In 2nd chain from hook work 1 SC. Work 1 SC into each of the remaining chains. (14 sts)

Row 2: CH 1 and turn. In first stitch from the hook work 1 SC under both loops. Work 1 SC into the back loop of each of the next 12 sts. Work 1 SC under both loops on the last stitch.

Rows 3 - 68: Repeat row 2. (Or to the width you need. Just end on an even number of rows.)

Mark stitch while you join the rounds using a tapestry needle. Return to stitch. Join with a slip stitch to the base row. You will now be working around sides of the band. CH 1. *Work 1 SC into the side of the next row. CH 1 and skip the next row, repeat from * around the sides and join with a SL ST. (68)

Round 2: CH 1 and turn. *DC into the top two loops of the SC, SC into the ch spaces. Repeat from * around. Join with a slip stitch, pulling through with Black. Leave White behind. (You'll come back around after the round and pick it up.)

Round 3: CH 1 and turn. *DC into the top two loops of the SC, SC into the top two loops of the DC. Repeat from * around. Join with a slip stitch, pulling through with White.

Rounds 4 - 22: Repeat rounds 2 and 3.

Round 23: (Decreasing stitches) *DC2TOG across the next 2 SC, skipping over the DC in the row below. SC into the next DC. Repeat from * around. Join with a slip stitch pulling through with Black.

Round 24: Repeat round 3, keeping in mind you are working the SC into the tops of the DCTOGs.

Round 25: Repeat round 23, decreasing the rounds further. You will have one set of DC, SC at the end of the round, work those normally. Slip stitch and pull through with Black.

Round 26: Repeat round 22.

Before tying off and finishing the hat, turn it inside out and decide which side of the hat you like the best. One side has a darker black appearance, the other white. It is subtle but you'll want to decide before you add the pom pom.

Tie off and with a tapestry needle, thread the yarn in and out of the stitches, cinching the top closed. Tie off and weave in the ends. Attach a pom pom.

-Tiffany

HOT PADS

SPRING STRIPES HOT PAD

YARN

Lily Sugar 'n Cream
The Original Yarn
(large skein) 100% cotton
113 g/4 oz, 184 m/200 yds

COLORS

For one hot pad
1 skein White
1 skein Tangerine, Aquamarine
or Rose Pink

HOOK

Size H/5.00mm hook

TOOLS

Tapestry needle
Scissors

SIZE

8 in x 9 in

STITCHES

Herringbone Half Double
Crochet (HHDC)
Half Double Slip Stitch
(HDSS)
Double Crochet (DC)
Front and Back Post Double
Crochet (FPDC & BPDC)

PATTERN

Chain 24 with Main Color.

Row 1: Starting in the 2nd chain from the hook, work 1 HHDC in each chain. CH 1 and turn. (23 st)

Row 2: Work 1 HHDC in each stitch across the row. On the last stitch, pull through with White. CH 1 and turn. (Don't cut Main Color.)

Row 3: Work 1 HDSS in each stitch across the row. CH 1 and turn.

Row 4: Work 1 HDSS in each stitch across the row. On the last stitch, work 1 HHDC and finish the stitch by pulling though the last two loops with Main Color. (Bring Main Color up from previous row so that it lays against side of your work; don't cut White yarn.) CH 1 and turn.

Row 5: Work 1 HHDC in each stitch across the row. CH 1 and turn.

Row 6: Work 1 HHDC in each stitch across the row. On the last stitch, pull through with White. (Bring White up from previous row so that it lays against side of your work.) CH 1 and turn.

Repeat rows 3 through 6 until you have six White stripes, and you end with 2 rows of HHDC in the Main Color.

Tie off and weave in ends, then start from beginning and make another square that is exactly the same.

BORDER

Place squares together so they are evenly lined up, with same sides facing each other. Pull up a loop in top left hand corner and chain 3. Work one round of DC around the hot pad, inserting your hook through both squares. Work 1 DC per row on the sides (2 DCs per white section and 2 DCs per color section) and 1 DC per stitch at the top and bottom of the hot pad. Work 3 DCs in each corner.

When you reach the starting corner, work 3 DCs into corner, then continue working in the same direction around the hot pad, this time alternating FPDC and BPDC. When you reach a corner, work 3 alternating FPDC and BPDC around the middle DC of the 3 DC that made the corner in the round prior. Slip stitch into the starting stitch and tie off.

-Hannah

STRIPED HEART HOT PAD

YARN

Lily Sugar 'n Cream
The Original Yarn
(small skein) 100% cotton
71 g/2.5 oz, 109 m/120 yds

COLORS

For one hot pad
1 skein Tea Rose
1 skein White

TOOLS

Size H/5.00mm hook
Tapestry needle
Scissors

SIZE

10 in x 10 in

GAUGE

4 in = 14 st, 12 rows HHDC

STITCHES

Herringbone Half Double
Crochet (HHDC)
Small Puff Stitch
Single Crochet (SC)
Half Double Crochet (HDC)

VIDEO

PATTERN

When using graph: the odd rows are read right to left, the even rows left to right.

Chain 27 with White.

Row 1: Starting in the 3rd chain from the hook, work 1 HHDC in each chain. CH 2 and turn. (25 st)

Row 2: *(Right side, keep all the ends to the wrong side of the work).* Work 1 HHDC in each of the next 12 stitches. Change color, work 1 HHDC, change color, 1 HHDC in each of the remaining 12 stitches. CH 2 and turn.

Row 3: 1 HHDC in each of the next 11 stitches. Change color, work 1 HHDC in each of the next 3 stitches. Change color, 1 HHDC in remaining 11 stitches. CH 2 and turn.

Row 4: 1 HHDC in each stitch across the row. CH 2 and turn.

Rows 5 - 21: Follow the graph making the color changes as needed.

Tip: Do not cut the yarn, leave the tail to the wrong side of the work and pull through when needed.

Before tying off, work one round of SC. Work 3 SC into each corner space, work 2 SC per the end of a row, skip a row, work 2 SC per stitch, skip a stitch. Join with a slip stitch to the starting SC, tie off. Make a solid color backing using the previous pattern, omitting color changes. Finish off with one round of SC as explained before.

BORDER

Place the two squares together with the wrong side facing in. Join the two squares in any corner with a slip stitch then work SC into each SC around. Join with a slip stitch to the first stitch, CH 2 and turn.

Work 1 *HDC into stitch. Work Small Puff stitch around the post of the HDC you just made. Skip one stitch, repeat from *.

When you get to the corners, omit skipping over one stitch. To finish the round, work final Puff stitch and join with a slip stitch to the first Puff of the round. Tie off and weave in ends.

-Tiffany

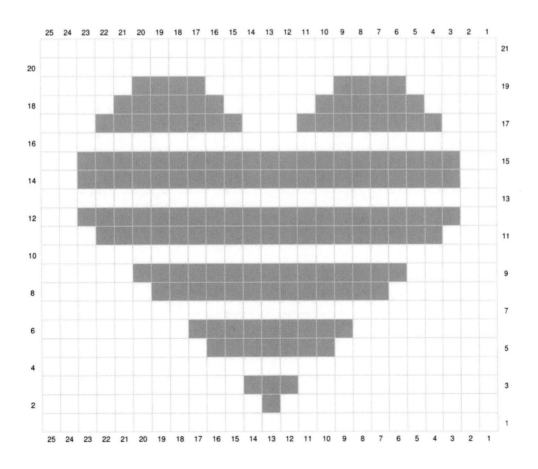

PICNIC GINGHAM HOT PADS

YARN

Lily Sugar 'n Cream
The Original Yarn
(small skein) 100% cotton
71 g/2.5 oz, 109 m/120 yds

COLORS

For orange gingham hot pad
1 skein Ecru (Main Color)
1 skein Tea Rose (Color A)
1 skein Tangerine (Color B)

For teal gingham hot pad
1 skein Ecru (Main Color)
1 skein Beach Glass (Color A)
1 skein Seabreeze (Color B)

TOOLS

Size H/5.00mm hook
Tapestry needle
Scissors

SIZE

7 in x 7 in

GAUGE

4 in = 14 st, 10 rows HDC

STITCHES

Half Double Crochet (HDC)

PATTERN

Changing colors: Pull through with the new color just before you finish the HDC stitch, when you still have three loops on your hook. Lay whichever color you aren't using across the top of your work and crochet over it until you are ready to use it again. To avoid your yarn getting twisted as you carry it along your work, it helps to always keep one color to the front and one color to the back each time you switch colors.

Chain 23 with Main Color.

Row 1: With Main Color, HDC in the 3rd chain from the hook, then HDC in each of the next 2 chains. *HDC in each of the next 3 chains with Color A, then HDC in each of the next 3 chains with Main Color, always crocheting over whichever color you aren't using and carrying it along your work. Repeat from * to the end of the row. CH 2 and turn (turning chain does not count as a stitch).

Row 2: Wrap Color A around the side of your work and crochet over it as you *HDC in each of the next 3 stitches with Main Color, then HDC in each of the next 3 stitches with Color A. Repeat from * to the end of the row. On the last stitch of the row, pull through with Color A. CH 2 and turn.

Row 3: *HDC in each of the next 3 stitches with Color A, then HDC in each of the next 3 stitches with Color B. Repeat from * to the end of the row. CH 2 and turn.

Row 4: Repeat row 3. On the last stitch of the row, pull through with Main Color, then CH 2 and turn.

Row 5: *HDC in each of the next 3 stitches with Main Color, then HDC in each of the next 3 stitches with Color A. Repeat from * to the end of the row. CH 2 and turn.

Row 6: *HDC in each of the next 3 stitches with Main Color, then HDC in each of the next 3 stitches with Color A. Repeat from * to the end of the row. On the last stitch of the row, pull through with Color A. CH 2 and turn.

Repeat rows 3 through 6 two more times.

When you finish the first square, tie off, weave in any ends and set it aside. Then make a second square, following the pattern from the beginning. When you have two squares, line them up evenly and place them together. Pull up a loop in the top left corner with Main Color, inserting your hook through both squares, and CH 2. Now, HDC around the edges of the squares, inserting your hook through both squares to stitch them together. Work 3 HDCs into each corner.

When you reach the corner you started with, slip stitch into the corner, CH 10, then slip stitch back into the same corner to make a loop. Tie off, and leave a long tail that you can wrap around the base of the loop a few times, then weave the tail into the hot pad to keep it secure. Weave in all ends.

-Hannah

BUNNY HOT PAD

YARN

Bernat Handicrafter Cotton
100% cotton
50 g/1.75 oz, 73 m/80 yds

COLORS

1 skein White
1 skein Robins Egg

TOOLS

Size H/5.00mm hook
Tapestry needle
Scissors

SIZE

8 in x 8 in

GAUGE

4 in = 15 st, 16 rows SC

STITCHES

Single Crochet (SC)
Double Crochet (DC)

PATTERN

Chain 27 with White.

Follow the graph from right to left on the odd-numbered rows, and left to right on the even-numbered rows. Each square represents 1 SC. Work SC into each chain, making the appropriate color changes. To change colors, pull through with new color on last step of the previous stitch. No need to cut the White, or carry along the row since all ends will be hidden in the middle of the hot pad. Always CH 1 and turn at the end of each row.

When finished with the graph, work one complete round of SC into each stitch, and at the end of each row, and work 3 SC into each corner. Join with a slip stitch to the first SC of the round, tie off. Make a second side in a solid color using same stitch and counts. Join the two sides with a round of SC. Matching the squares together, work SC into each stitch inserting your hook through both squares to join them together. Work 3 SC into each corner. Join to the starting SC and CH 2.

Continue in the same direction, begin the round with 2 DC into the space where you joined the round. *SK two stitches, work 1 SC into the next stitch. SK 2 stitches, 5 DC into the next stitch. Repeat from * around. (On the corners, skip only one stitch if needed.) At the end of the round, estimate if you need to skip one or two stitches in between the shells and SC. Finish the round with 2 DC into the starting chain space. Slip stitch into the top of the starting chain to join, tie off and weave in the ends.

-Tiffany

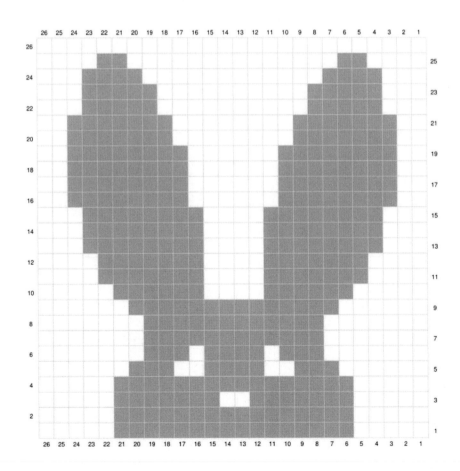

FALL COLORS TEXTURED HOT PADS

YARN

Bernat Softee Cotton
60% cotton, 40% acrylic
120 g/4.2 oz, 232 m/254 yds

COLORS

For one hot pad
1 skein Pool Green, Seaside Blue
or Sandstone

TOOLS

Size H/5.00mm hook
Tapestry needle
Scissors

SIZE

8 in x 8 in

GAUGE

4 in = 13 st, 13 rows pattern

STITCHES

Single Crochet (SC)
Double Crochet 4 Together
(DC4TOG) Bobble
Treble Crochet
Berry Stitch
Double Crochet (DC)
Front and Back Post Double
Crochet (FPDC & BPDC)

VIDEO

PATTERN

Chain 22.

Row 1: Starting in the 2nd chain from the hook, work 1 SC into each chain. CH 1 and turn.

Row 2: Work 1 SC into the first stitch, then 1 Bobble into the next stitch. *Work 1 SC into the next stitch, then 1 Bobble into the next stitch. Repeat from * across the row, ending with 1 SC in the last stitch. CH 1 and turn.

Row 3: Work 1 SC into each stitch across the row. CH 1 and turn.

Repeat rows 2 through 3 until you have 21 rows total, then tie off. Set square aside and repeat instructions from beginning to make a second square.

For variations of this pattern, try subbing a Bobble for a Treble Crochet or Berry Stitch.

BORDER

You can either weave in ends before beginning border, or simply hide them in the middle of your hot pad when you place the two squares together.

Round 1: Place squares together so they are evenly lined up, with the textured sides facing outward. Pull up a loop in top left hand corner and CH 3. Work one round of DC around the hot pad, inserting your hook through both squares. Work 21 DC along each of the sides and 3 DC in each corner space.

Round 2: Work 3 DCs into starting corner, then continue working in the same direction around the hot pad, this time alternating FPDC and BPDC. When you reach a corner, work 3 alternating FPDC and BPDC around the middle DC of the 3 DC that made the corner in the round prior.

Round 3: Continue working in same direction and repeat round 2, making sure that post DCs are popping out in same direction as previous row. When you reach a corner, work 3 alternating FPDC and BPDC around the middle DC post of the 3 DC that made the corner in the round prior. Slip stitch into the starting stitch and tie off, then weave in ends with a tapestry needle.

-Hannah

TREE STRIPE HOT PAD

YARN

Lily Sugar 'n Cream
The Original Yarn
(small skein) 100% cotton
71 g/2.5 oz, 109 m/120 yds

COLORS

1 skein Sage Green
1 skein White

TOOLS

Size H/5.00mm hook
Tapestry needle
Scissors

SIZE

8 in x 8.5 in

GAUGE

4 in = 14 st, 12 rows pattern

STITCHES

Herringbone Half Double
Crochet (HHDC)
Single Crochet (SC)
Dot

PATTERN

Graph is read as odd rows right to left, the even rows are left to right. All color changes happen on odd rows.

Chain 28 with White.

Row 1: Work 1 HHDC in the 3rd chain from the hook. Work 1 HHDC in each chain across the row. CH 2 and turn. (26 st)

Row 2: *Turning chain does not count as a stitch.* Work 1 HHDC into the first stitch. 1 HHDC in each stitch across the row. CH 2 and turn.

Row 3: 1 HHDC in the first 3 stitches in White, change to Sage Green, 1 HHDC in each of the next 20 stitches, (crochet over the White tail, laying it across the row as you work the green stitches) change to White, (leave the green tail behind, do not cut or crochet over it). 1 HHDC in each of the remaining 3 stitches. CH 2 and turn.

Row 4 and all even rows going forward: Repeat row 2.

Row 5: 1 HHDC in each of the first 4 stitches in White, change to Sage Green, 1 HHDC in each of the next 18 stitches, change to White, 1 HHDC in each of the remaining 4 stitches, CH 2 and turn.

Row 7: 1 HHDC in each of the first 5 stitches in White, change to Sage Green, 1 HHDC in each of the next 16 stitches. Change to White, 1 HHDC in each of the remaining 5 stitches. CH 2 and turn.

Row 9: 1 HHDC in each of the first 6 stitches in White, change to Sage Green, 1 HHDC in each of the next 14 stitches. Change to White, 1 HHDC in each of the remaining 6 stitches. CH 2 and turn.

Row 11: 1 HHDC in each of the first 7 stitches in White, change to Sage Green, 1 HHDC in each of the next 12 stitches. Change to White, 1 HHDC in each of the remaining 7 stitches. CH 2 and turn.

Row 13: 1 HHDC in each of the first 8 stitches in White, change to Sage Green, 1 HHDC in each of the next 10 stitches. Change to White, 1 HHDC in each of the remaining 8 stitches. CH 2 and turn.

Row 15: 1 HHDC in each of the first 9 stitches in White, change to Sage Green, 1 HHDC in each of the next 8 stitches. Change to White, 1 HHDC in each of the remaining 9 stitches. CH 2 and turn.

Row 17: 1 HHDC in each of the first 10 stitches in White, change to Sage Green, 1 HHDC in each of the next 6 stitches. Change to White, 1 HHDC in each of the remaining 10 stitches. CH 2 and turn.

Row 19: 1 HHDC in each of the first 11 stitches in White, change to Sage Green. 1 HHDC in each of the next 4 stitches. Change to White, 1 HHDC in each of the remaining 11 stitches. CH 2 and turn.

Row 21: 1 HHDC in each of the first 12 stitches in White, change to Sage Green. 1 HHDC in each of the next 2 stitches. Change to White, 1 HHDC in each of the remaining 12 stitches. CH 2 and turn.

Rows 22 - 23: With White work 2 rows of HHDC. Always CH 2 and turn. Don't cut White, continue to border.

Tree Side Border: CH 1 and turn. Work 1 SC in the first stitch. *Skip the next stitch, work 2 SC into the next stitch. Repeat from * across the top, work 3 SC into the corner. Rotate the hot pad and work the side by working 2 SC around the turning chains only. Work 3 SC into the corner. Rotate the hot pad and work across the bottom of starting chain by working 2 SC into the first space, skipping the next and working 2 SC into the next.

Work 3 SC into the corner, rotate the hot pad one last time to work the final side in the same manner as the first. Only work 2 SC around the chain 2 turning chains. Work 2 SC into the final corner and join with a slip stitch to the first stitch of the round. Tie off and weave in all the ends.

Back of Hot Pad: Chain 28 with Sage Green.

Row 1: Starting in the 3rd chain from the hook, work 1 HHDC in each chain. CH 2 and turn.

Rows 2 - 23: Work HHDC in each stitch, CH 2 and turn.

Back of Hot Pad Border: Work in the same manner as before, but don't tie off. You'll use Sage Green to SC the two squares together.

Combining Squares: With the Winter Tree right side facing you, place the green square behind. Take your hook out of the green loop, insert it through the white corner, then grab the loop and pull through. YO and pull through slip stitching the two together.

Now work SC under each color of stitches, joining them together. Work 3 SC in each corner. In the final corner, work 3 SC and join with a slip stitch to the first SC. Do not turn.

DOT BORDER

**CH 2. In the first chain, *YO and insert your hook, YO and pull up a loop. Repeat from * 3 more times. YO and pull through all loops on your hook. Slip stitch into the stitch just below the chain 2 to secure the puff. Slip stitch into each of the next 4 stitches. Repeat from ** around.

Join with a slip stitch to the first stitch, tie off and weave in all ends.

-Tiffany

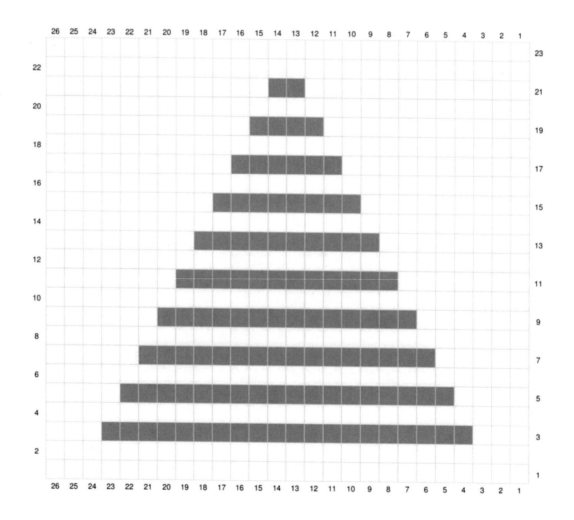

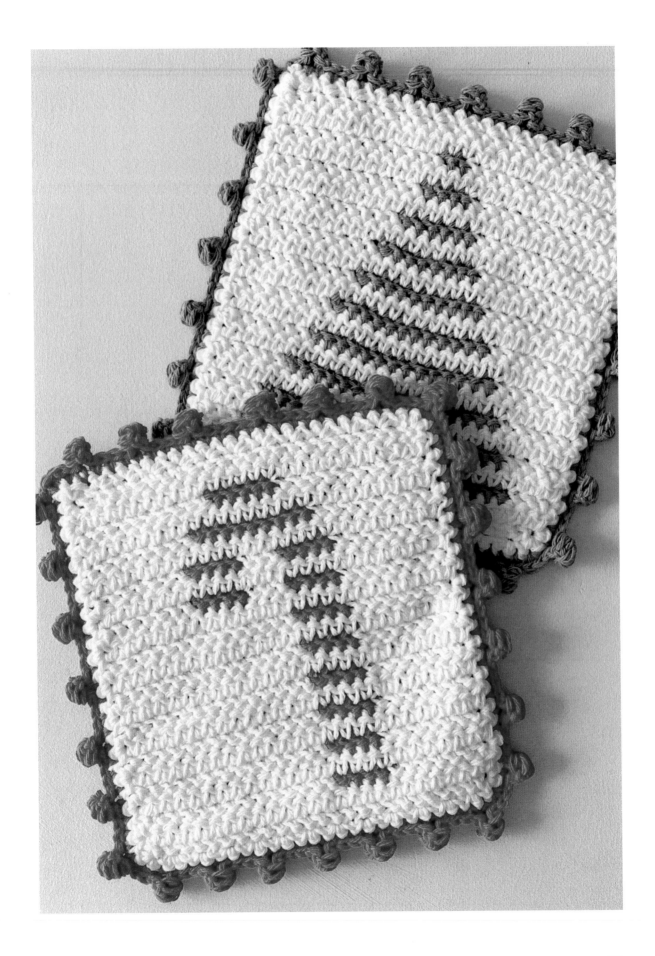

CANDY CANE HOT PAD

YARN

Lily Sugar 'n Cream
The Original Yarn
(small skein) 100% cotton
71 g/2.5 oz, 109 m/120 yds

COLORS

1 skein Red
1 skein White

TOOLS

Size H/5.00mm hook
Tapestry needle
Scissors

SIZE

8 in x 8.5 in

GAUGE

4 in = 14 st, 12 rows HHDC

STITCHES

Herringbone Half Double
Crochet (HHDC)
Single Crochet (SC)
Dot

VIDEO

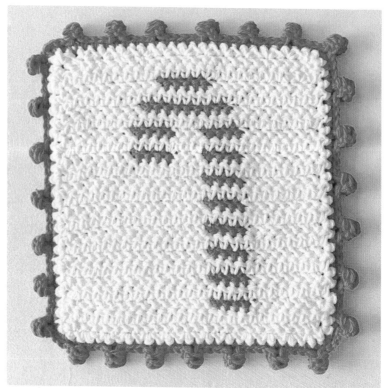

PATTERN

Graph is read as odd rows right to left, even rows left to right. All color changes happen on odd rows.

Chain 27 with White.

Row 1: Work 1 HHDC in the 3rd chain from the hook. Work 1 HHDC in each chain across the row. CH 2 and turn. (25 st)

Row 2: *The turning chain does not count as a stitch.* Work 1 HHDC into the first stitch. 1 HHDC in each stitch across the row. CH 2 and turn.

Row 3: 1 HHDC in the first 7 stitches in White, change to Red, 1 HHDC in each of the next 4 stitches, (crochet over the White tail, laying it across the row as you work the Red stitches) change to White, (leave the Red tail behind, do not cut or crochet over it). 1 HHDC in each of the remaining 14 stitches. CH 2 and turn.

Rows 4 - 14: Repeat rows 2 and 3 and following the graph. Always CH 2 and turn. Also, keep the red tail to the back side of the work and pull it across when you need to change color. This will not be seen as the hot pad is double-sided and will be hidden on the inside of the hot pad when you join.

Row 15: 1 HHDC in each of the first 7 stitches in White, change to Red, 1 HHDC in each of the next 4 stitches, change to White, 1 HHDC in each of the next 3 stitches, change to Red, 1 HHDC in each of the next 4 stitches, change to White, 1 HHDC in each of the next 7 stitches. CH 2 and turn.

Row 16: Repeat row 2 instructions.

Row 17: Repeat row 15 instructions.

Row 18: Repeat row 2 instructions.

Row 19: 1 HHDC in each of the first 8 stitches in White, change to Red. 1 HHDC in each of the next 9 stitches. Change to White, 1 HHDC in each of the remaining 8 stitches, CH 2 and turn.

Row 20: Repeat row 2 instructions.

Row 21: 1 HHDC in each of the first 10 stitches. Change to Red, 1 HHDC in each of the next 5 stitches. Change to White. 1 HHDC in each of the remaining 10 stitches. CH 2 and turn.

Rows 22 - 23: Repeat row 2 instructions. Cut Red. Continue in White for the border.

Candy Cane Side Border: CH 1 and turn. Work 1 SC in the first stitch. *Skip the next st, work 2 SC into the next stitch. Repeat from * across the top, work 3 SC into the corner. Rotate the hot pad and work the side by working 2 SC around the turning chains only. Work 3 SC into the corner. Rotate the hot pad and work across the bottom of starting chain by working 2 SC into the first space, skipping the next and working 2 SC into the next. Work 3 SC into the corner, rotate the hot pad one last time to work the final side in the same manner as the first. Only work 2 SC around the turning chains. Work 2 SC into the final corner and join with a slip stitch to the first stitch of the round. Tie off and weave in all the ends.

Back of Hot Pad: Chain 27 with Red.

Row 1: Starting in the 3rd chain from the hook, work 1 HHDC in each chain. CH 2 and turn.

Rows 2 - 23: Work 1 HHDC in each stitch, CH 2 and turn.

Back of Hot Pad Border: Work in the same manner as before, but don't tie off. You'll use Red to SC the two squares together.

Combining Squares: With the Candy Cane right side facing you, place the red square behind. Take your hook out of the red loop, insert it through the white corner, then grab the loop and pull through. YO and pull through slip stitching the two together. Now work SC under each color of stitches, joining them together. Work 3 SC in each corner. In the final corner, work 3 SC and join with a slip stitch to the first SC. Do not turn.

DOT BORDER

**CH 2. In the first chain, *YO and insert your hook, YO and pull up a loop. Repeat from * 3 more times. YO and pull through all loops on your hook. Slip stitch into the stitch just below the chain 2 to secure the puff. Slip stitch into each of the next 4 stitches. Repeat from ** around. Join with a slip stitch to the first stitch, tie off and weave in all ends.

-Tiffany

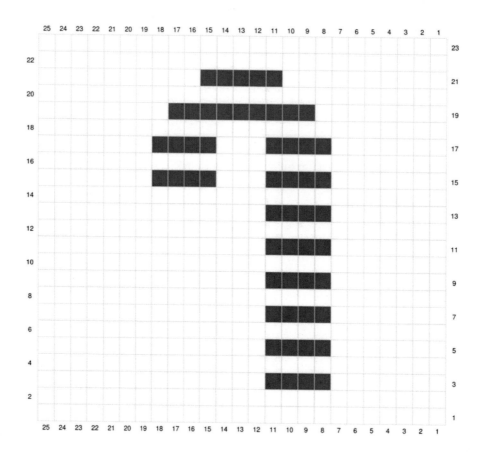

CHRISTMAS TREE PUFF HOT PAD

YARN

Lily Sugar 'n Cream
The Original Yarn
(large skein) 100% cotton
113 g/4 oz, 184 m/200 yds

COLORS

For one hot pad
1 skein Teal or Ecru

TOOLS

Size H/5.00mm hook
Tapestry needle
Scissors

SIZE

7.5 in x 8.5 in

GAUGE

4 in = 13 st, 11 rows HDC

STITCHES

Half Double Crochet (HDC)
Small Puff Stitch

VIDEO

PATTERN

Chain 23.

Row 1: Starting in the 3rd chain from the hook, work 1 HDC in each chain. CH 2 and turn (turning chain does not count as a stitch).

Row 2: Work 1 HDC in each of the first 2 stitches, then * 1 Small Puff in the next stitch, and 1 HDC in the next stitch. Repeat from * 7 times. Then work 1 Puff into the next stitch, and end the row with HDC in the last 2 stitches. CH 2 and turn.

Row 3: Work 1 HDC into each stitch across the row. CH 2 and turn.

Row 4: Work 1 HDC in each of the first 3 stitches, then *1 Puff in the next stitch, and 1 HDC in the next stitch. Repeat from * 6 times. Then work 1 Puff into the next stitch, and end the row with HDC in the last 3 stitches. CH 2 and turn.

Row 5: Work 1 HDC into each stitch across the row. CH 2 and turn.

Row 6: Work 1 HDC in each of the first 4 stitches, then *1 Puff in the next stitch, and 1 HDC in the next stitch. Repeat from * 5 times. Then work 1 Puff into the next stitch, and end the row with HDC in the last 4 stitches. CH 2 and turn.

Row 7: Work 1 HDC into each stitch across the row. CH 2 and turn.

Row 8: Work 1 HDC in each of the first 5 stitches, then *1 Puff in the next stitch, and 1 HDC in the next stitch. Repeat from * 4 times. Then work 1 Puff into the next stitch, and end the row with HDC in the last 5 stitches. CH 2 and turn.

Row 9: Work 1 HDC into each stitch across the row. CH 2 and turn.

Row 10: Work 1 HDC in each of the first 6 stitches, then *1 Puff in the next stitch, and 1 HDC in the next stitch. Repeat from * 3 times. Then work 1 Puff into the next stitch, and end the row with HDC in the last 6 stitches. CH 2 and turn.

Row 11: Work 1 HDC into each stitch across the row. CH 2 and turn.

Row 12: Work 1 HDC in each of the first 7 stitches, then *1 Puff in the next stitch, and 1 HDC in the next stitch. Repeat from * 2 times. Then work 1 Puff into the next stitch, and end the row with HDC in the last 7 stitches. CH 2 and turn.

Row 13: Work 1 HDC into each stitch across the row. CH 2 and turn.

Row 14: Work 1 HDC in each of the first 8 stitches, then *1 Puff in the next stitch, and 1 HDC in the next stitch. Repeat from * one time. Then work 1 Puff into the next stitch, and end the row with HDC in the last 8 stitches. CH 2 and turn.

Row 15: Work 1 HDC into each stitch across the row. CH 2 and turn.

Row 16: Work 1 HDC in each of the first 9 stitches, then 1 Puff in the next stitch, and 1 HDC in the next stitch. Then work 1 Puff into the next stitch, and end the row with HDC in the last 9 stitches. CH 2 and turn.

Row 17: Work 1 HDC into each stitch across the row. CH 2 and turn.

Row 18: Work 1 HDC in each of the first 10 stitches, then 1 Puff in the next stitch. Work 1 HDC in each of the next 10 stitches. CH 2 and turn.

Row 19: Work 1 HDC into each stitch across the row. CH 1 and tie off.

Second square: CH 23 and work 19 rows of HDC.

BORDER

Combine squares and with the puffs facing toward you, pull up a loop in the top left hand corner and CH 2. Insert your hook through both sides of each square and work 1 HDC per row on the sides, and 1 HDC per stitch on the ends. Work 3 HDCs into each corner. Slip stitch into starting chain and CH 10. Then slip stitch into the corner again and tie off. Wrap your tail around the bottom of the chain 10 a few times before weaving it into the hot pad.

-Hannah

Thank you for being our crochet friends!
xo, Tiffany and Hannah

Find all of our free crochet patterns on
daisyfarmcrafts.com

Follow us on Instagram, Facebook and Pinterest
@daisyfarmcrafts

Find all of our free video tutorials on the
Daisy Farm Crafts YouTube Channel

Made in the USA
Middletown, DE
01 July 2023

34380963R00075